MY MOTHER
and me

Thomas Hauser

ADMISSION PRESS

www.admissionpress.com

Books by Thomas Hauser

General Non-Fiction

Missing

The Trial of Patrolman Thomas Shea

For Our Children (with Frank Macchiarola)

Final Warning: The Legacy of Chernobyl (with Dr. Robert Gale)

Arnold Palmer: A Personal Journey

Confronting America's Moral Crisis (with Frank Macchiarola)

Healing: A Journal of Tolerance and Understanding
(with Muhammad Ali)

With This Ring (with Frank Macchiarola)

Thomas Hauser on Sports

Reflections

My Mother and me

Boxing Non-Fiction

The Black Lights: Inside the World of Professional Boxing

Muhammad Ali: His Life and Times

Muhammad Ali: Memories

Muhammad Ali: In Perspective

Muhammad Ali & Company

A Beautiful Sickness

A Year At The Fights

Brutal Artistry

The View From Ringside

Chaos, Corruption, Courage, and Glory

I Don't Believe It, But It's True

Knockout (with Vikki LaMotta)

The Greatest Sport of All

The Boxing Scene

An Unforgiving Sport

Boxing Is . . .

Box: The Face of Boxing

The Legend of Muhammad Ali (with Bart Barry)

Winks and Daggers

And the New . . .

Straight Writes and Jabs

Thomas Hauser on Boxing

A Hurting Sport

A Hard World

Muhammad Ali: A Tribute to the Greatest

There Will Always Be Boxing

Protect Yourself At All Times

A Dangerous Journey

Staredown

Broken Dreams

In the Inner Sanctum

The Universal Sport

Fiction

Ashworth & Palmer

Agatha's Friends

The Beethoven Conspiracy

Hanneman's War

The Fantasy

Dear Hannah

The Hawthorne Group

Mark Twain Remembers

Finding The Princess

Waiting For Carver Boyd

The Final Recollections of Charles Dickens

The Baker's Tale

For Children

Martin Bear & Friends

MY MOTHER
and me

by Thomas Hauser

This book is dedicated to my mother
and to all the people who helped make her life
as fulfilling as it was.

Chapter I

I've known for years that I would write this book. I wanted my mother to have this marker. But I didn't want to begin writing while she was alive. That would have meant writing each day with the shadow of her death in my mind.

So I waited.

My mother was ninety-six years old when she died. She lived a long, privileged life and died at home, which was where she wanted to be. I arrived at her apartment a half hour later, called 911, and told the operator that my mother was dead.

New York City has a checklist of things that have to be done when a death is reported . . . Two emergency medical technicians came to her apartment . . . Shortly before they left, two police officers arrived.

I called my mother's internist (who had known her health was failing). He'd promised that, when the time came, he would call the Medical Examiner's Office and ask that they waive the requirement that her body be autopsied at the morgue so she could be sent directly to the funeral home.

A homicide detective came to the apartment and interviewed me. He asked what medications my mother had been taking and looked at some pill bottles. The inquiry, he explained, was necessary because my mother had died at home and was not in hospice care.

I don't remember what any of the people who came to the apartment that afternoon looked like. Some of what happened that day will be etched in my mind forever. Some is blurred.

I spoke by telephone with the Medical Examiner's Office.

A team from Riverside Memorial Chapel arrived at the apartment and removed my mother's body.

There were calls to family and friends.

I'd thought I would begin writing this book as soon as my mother died. A week passed. Then a month. Too much else was going on . . . Canceling her credit cards and closing bank accounts . . . Answering condolence letters . . . Emptying out her apartment . . . The administration of her estate . . . The other parts of my life . . .

I wanted time to sit back and reflect before I began.

My mother knew I'd be writing this book. "And I want you to be honest," she'd told me. "Don't make me out to be a saint. You should put in the things I did wrong too."

"And the affairs were part of our marriage," she added. "You can write about them too. It wouldn't be much of a book if you left them out."

My brother and sister aren't talked about at length in the pages that follow. That's not to minimize their role in my mother's life. Rather, they're entitled to their own recounting and interpretation of her narrative.

I knew my mother first from the perspective of a young child. Then as an adolescent, an adult and, finally, as a mature adult. I was fortunate to have had her though all those stages of my life. The more she aged, the more time I spent with her and the better we came to know each other. We came to see each other not just as mother and son—although that was always at the core of our relationship—but as people with identities that went beyond our mother-son bond.

Her story is the story of relationships as they emerged and changed over time—some new and some old, some casual, some familial, some romantic.

If she'd been born in today's world, she might have risen through the ranks at a financial institution or philanthropic foundation. But she grew up in an era when few women from financially comfortable families had careers—particularly not women who were beautiful and married at age nineteen.

"None of my friends from adolescence or the early years of my marriage had a career," she told me. "It's hard to put yourself in another generation, so I can't say what would have happened if I'd been born later. In my generation, the goal was to get married."

She was a "city girl" who spent four decades living in the suburbs.

She was a conscientious parent and carried the family through a harrowing eight years when my father was debilitated by depression.

She experienced soaring highs and hard falls.

She deconstructed and rebuilt her life several times.

Her character evolved from a self-described "selfish" woman to someone with a deep well of empathy for others.

She was a remarkable conversationalist. One reason for that is she was verbally gifted and knowledgeable on a wide range of subjects. She had a thirst for knowledge and never stopped learning. But equally important, she was genuinely interested in other people, who they were and what they had to say. When she asked someone about his or her life, she genuinely wanted to know the answer.

She empathized with other people's struggles. She believed

that "little people" were entitled to as much opportunity, dignity, and respect as "big" ones.

She was strong-willed and a sentimental mush.

She had a wonderful sense of humor and laughed out loud at things she found funny but rarely told jokes.

Late in life, she was happy and felt completely fulfilled.

She grew old gracefully and met the struggles of old age without complaint. In her final years, she was content and serene.

There came a time when she felt that she had lived long enough and was ready to die.

I've tried to write her story in a way that reflects how I see her and how she saw herself.

My mother's father kept a scrapbook filled with family photographs, marriage contracts, death certificates, and other documents that date back to the mid-nineteenth century. He bequeathed it to her when he died. The pages have grown brittle with the passage of time. Pieces break off when I turn them. One of my mother's maternal aunts researched another branch of the family tree, typed up her findings, and made several carbon-paper copies.

These histories are a good place to start in understanding my mother. She felt connected to the names and faces in them. Her feeling of family reached back to a time long before she was born.

My mother's maiden name was Eleanor Nordlinger. For ninety-six years, she was known as Ellie. Her paternal ancestors were German Jews who lived in a town called Nordlingen. The oldest photograph in my grandfather's scrapbook shows an old man and woman surrounded by family. They are David

Nordlinger and Babette Ottinger Nordlinger (my mother's great-great-grandparents). The photo was taken on June 13, 1870—their fiftieth wedding anniversary. Three months later, David Nordlinger (who'd been born in 1794) died. Babette, six years younger, lived until 1875.

One of the young men in the photograph was their son, Henry Nordlinger. Henry had come to New York in 1850 at age twenty-one and set up a business importing dried fruit, coffee, and sugar to America. His son (Edwin Henry Nordlinger) graduated from the City College of New York and joined his father at Nordlinger & Co. Edwin married a woman named Henriette Bacharach, who had spent her early years in France before coming to America with her parents.

Edwin and Henriette had one child—Henry Harold Nordlinger, my mother's father.

The maternal side of my mother's family had roots that stretched even deeper into American soil.

Moses Reis (my mother's great-great-great-grandfather) was born in Alsace Lorraine in 1770. He and his wife came to the United States with their five children in 1833 and settled in New Orleans. Their granddaughter, Ellen Emsheimer was born in 1837 and moved with her parents to Natchez, Mississippi. At age fifteen, Ellen married Lehman Lehrburger, who had come to the United States from Germany in the 1840s. Eventually, they settled in Geneva, New York, where their first child (Simon Lehrburger) was born.

Simon was a traveling salesman who represented wholesale houses and sold dress trimmings (lace, braids, and other ornaments) throughout New England. At age thirty-one, looking to improve his circumstances, he co-founded a company called Lehrburger & Asher that manufactured and sold fur coats in Boston. The following year, 1891, he married Mathilda (Tilly)

Frank whose grandparents had come to the United States from Germany in the 1850s.

Simon and Tilly Lehrburger had four children, including Elise Lehrburger (my mother's mother).

That's the cliff notes version of my mother's ancestry. Other than her parents, the only person mentioned in the preceding paragraphs who she knew was her grandmother Henriette (who died when my mother was six years old).

The family history becomes more vibrant for me when it reaches my mother's parents. I knew them well.

My grandfather was born in 1893. Throughout his life, he was known as Harry. He grew up in a New York City apartment with his parents and his mother's three sisters—Martha, Florence, and Blanche. Blanche never married. The other sisters did.

My grandfather had a remarkable mind with a particular gift for analytical thinking and mathematics. He was offered a faculty position after he graduated from college at Columbia but went to Columbia Law School instead. Later, he founded a small law firm that survived for decades. He very much wanted to be a judge and would have been a good one. He was smart, hard-working, and had absolute integrity.

A friend once told him, "Harry, you're very honest." My grandfather replied, "There's no such thing as very honest. Either you're honest or you're not."

But he didn't know how to play the political game and never came close to becoming a judge.

Sometime around 1960, my grandfather's law firm hired a temporary secretary when one of the women (the lawyers were all men, and the secretaries were all women) was out of the office for several weeks. The temp didn't get along with the other secretaries, who went as a group to my grandfather and asked him to fire her. The issue became moot when the temp left of her own accord. Several years later, my grandfather saw her on *The Tonight Show* and looked at the firm's old employment records to make sure it was the same person. Her name was Barbra Streisand.

My grandfather was admirably open to new ideas and curious about them. He evinced a wide range of intellectual interests from opera and astronomy to literature and Norse mythology. If someone asked him what time it was, he might have responded with a ten-minute exposition on how to make a watch. But one could be certain that the time referenced in his answer would be accurate.

His photograph is in the 1913 Columbia yearbook. The activities and accomplishments listed beside it include participation in the Class Debating Society, the Philharmonic Society (he played the violin), and the Boar's Head Society (which was devoted to reading and discussing poetry). His honors included induction into Phi Beta Kappa and being awarded an honor called the Van Buren Prize in Mathematics. Above his name, the yearbook editors saw fit to insert the legend, "Nordy. His intellect is improperly exposed."

My grandmother (Elise) was born in 1903, the last of Simon and Tilly Lehrburger's four children. She had two older brothers (Richard and Lyman) who everyone in the family adored. A fourth child (Alan) had been born in 1899 and died at age two after contracting pneumonia. Early deaths were common in those days. Tilly died of pernicious anemia in 1916 after a long debilitating illness.

My grandmother went to Simmons College in Boston for a year, then transferred to Teachers College at Columbia in New York. She never graduated. She and my grandfather met on a blind date. He had proposed marriage to six women (each of whom declined) prior to proposing to my grandmother. She accepted and they were married on November 8, 1924.

My grandmother was happiest when she felt needed and was helping others. She was devoted to family and friends. She made no pretense of being an intellectual. She and my grandfather were remarkably different from each other. At times, their only compatibility seemed to be at the bridge table. He played a mathematical game. She had exceptionally good intuition when it came to cards.

They were married for fifty-one years. Decades after their passing, it's impossible for me to think at length about one of them without thinking about the other.

My mother was born on December 28, 1925. Prohibition was the law of the land. Earlier that year, a biology teacher named John Scopes had been tried and convicted for the crime of teaching Darwin's theory of evolution to students in Tennessee. Penicillin as a weapon against bacterial infection was unknown. The stock market was booming. Americans were buying houses and automobiles in record numbers. The "Roaring Twenties" were in full bloom.

Meanwhile, overseas, Joseph Stalin was consolidating his power after the death of Vladimir Lenin. And Adolph Hitler published *Mein Kampf*.

My grandparents were financially comfortable. Old documents indicate that Edwin Nordlinger's assets were valued at $295,216 at the time of his death in 1926 (slightly more than $5,000,000 in today's dollars). One-third of that went outright to my grandfather (Edwin's son). The rest was placed in trust for Edwin's wife with the principle going to my grandfather after she died. The family weathered the stock market crash of 1929 reasonably well and my grandparents had two more children—a daughter (Ruth) born in 1930 and a son (Edwin) in 1934.

During the first year of my mother's life, she and her parents lived in an apartment on 87th Street between Amsterdam and Columbus Avenues on the west side of Manhattan. Then they moved to Broadway and West 86th Street. In late-1931, construction was completed on a massive 30-story art deco building on Central Park West between 71st and 72nd Streets. Unlike many of New York's "better" residences, The Majestic wasn't "restricted." In other words, it accepted Jews as tenants. My grandparents moved into apartment 14D.

The apartment was huge with a sunken living room, wood-burning fireplace, dining room, three bedrooms, four bathrooms, kitchen, two small maids' rooms off the kitchen, and large foyer. After my uncle was born, my mother shared a bedroom with her younger sister.

My mother was six when the family moved to The Majestic. The change in surroundings delighted her. Several months earlier, the 20-month-old son of Charles and Ann Morrow Lindbergh had been abducted from their New Jersey home. A homemade ladder was found beneath the child's second-floor bedroom window. The Lindberghs paid a $50,000 ransom. Ten weeks after the kidnapping, their son's body was found in a wooded area four miles from their home.

"The Crime of the Century" captivated America. Charles Lindbergh was a national hero, the first man to have flown solo non-stop across the Atlantic Ocean. My grandparents' previous apartment had been on the fourth floor, and my mother was terrified that someone would climb up a ladder at night and kidnap her. Fourteen was safer than four.

A German national named Bruno Hauptmann was arrested,

tried for the kidnapping, found guilty, and executed. The evidence presented against him at trial included $14,600 from the ransom payment (which was found in his garage) and similarities between his handwriting and the handwriting in the ransom notes. Also, Hauptmann had been absent from work on the day that the ransom payment was made. That's relevant here because Hauptmann had begun working at The Majestic (my mother's new "safe" home) as a carpenter two weeks after the kidnapping and quit his job two days after the ransom payment was collected.

My mother was an inquisitive child. And she loved books.

"One of the best things my mother ever did for me," she said years later, "was take me to the library when I was young and let me pick out books that we brought home and read together."

That love of learning was nurtured further in school. My mother attended the Ethical Culture School a few blocks from her home for grades one through six. Then she graduated to Fieldston, a private school in the Riverdale section of the Bronx.

Fieldston taught students about Plato and Aristotle and also automobile mechanics. There was a heavy dose of ethics with emphasis on the need for social justice and the obligation that the young men and women who attended Fieldston owed to society. It's not enough to just learn values, students were told. These values have to become part of who you are.

Fieldston was important to my mother. The years she spent there broadened her horizons intellectually and were among the happiest of her life.

Part of that joy came from discovering boys.

"I was a rule–breaker when it came to boys," she later acknowledged.

Other rules were broken too.

My mother was suspended from school three times: once

for cutting classes to go to the movies, once for smoking in the girls' lavatory, and once for using a Latin-to-English guide to facilitate her homework in Latin class.

She was three weeks shy of sixteen and in eleventh grade when the Japanese bombed Pearl Harbor and the United States entered World War II.

"To have our Pacific fleet wiped out when we weren't even at war was hard to understand," she said, looking back on that era. "And it wasn't certain that we'd win the war. It was a very scary time."

But the optimism of youth was on her side.

During those years, my mother developed a lifelong attachment to Frank Sinatra. At age seventeen, she was one of the bobbysoxers at his breakthrough engagement at The Paramount Theatre in Times Square. Decades later, she reminisced, "I didn't scream, but there was a lot of screaming. It was exciting, sort of like a fever. Like every other girl there that day, I thought he was singing just to me. I was crazy about him then, and I'm still crazy about him. Even now, when I hear him sing, it does something to me. I'm in my nineties. I can hardly walk. But when I hear Frank singing 'You Make Me Feel So Young,' I get up and dance."

At Fieldston, my mother also found young love. She and Bernard Nossiter (known then as Buddy) were listed alphabetically one right after the other in their graduating class. They "went steady" and didn't hide their fondness for one another. One of their teachers (Elbert Lenrow) inscribed my mother's senior yearbook with the sentiment, "I guess I did wrong to separate you and Bud in Eng VI, but it was probably best for all three of us. You were the belle of VI."

Other fading inscriptions in my mother's copy of the 1943 *Fieldglass* include one from a classmate named Patricia Brown ("Ellie dear, Always two cigarettes in the dark! Love and lots of the very best luck. Pat"). And another from a friend named Babette Brandt ("To the only girl who is willing and able to get into as much trouble as I am, Love, Babby").

My mother was blessed with the unearned privilege of good looks. She was uncommonly pretty, which occasioned attention. In her entire life, only one boy ever broke up with her. She was also the only girl in her high school economics class. Thus, Steve Lieber wrote in her yearbook, "To Ellie, the guiding light of feminine good sense and sweetness in that mess of vulgar males." Another paean came from Zachary Rosenfield (the class valedictorian) who noted, "Your proximity in chem recitation inspired me no end."

Buddy, who would be going to Dartmouth the following year, penned his inscription in green ink (Dartmouth's school color): "There's too damn much to encompass in the space and time that we have left. This ink reminds me of Dartmouth. And at the moment, that isn't a particularly happy thought. I'll miss you, darling, after six perfect years. You know that. All my love, Buddy."

My mother graduated from Fieldston in 1943. Some members of her graduating class went off to war. She went to Wellesley. And hated it.

"I'd gone to a high school where I had wonderful teachers and was surrounded by boys," she told me years later. "I had lousy teachers at Wellesley. There were no boys at Wellesley. I'm neat and my roommate was a slob."

At Wellesley, she also encountered antisemitism for the first time. Religion had never played a significant role in her life. My mother's parents believed in what they called cultural Jewish values. With a few minor exceptions, the rituals of Judaism weren't observed at home. Christmas was celebrated as a secular family holiday.

At Wellesley, my mother was shunned by some classmates

because of her religion and subjected to snide comments by others. One of the few pleasures she had there was walking into town every Friday afternoon, buying three jelly donuts, bringing them back to her dormitory room, and eating them.

She saw Buddy from time to time. But Dartmouth was four hours away. And at the end of his freshman year, he was drafted into the Army.

"I did well in economics and badly in everything else," my mother said of her time at Wellesley. "After my freshman year, I told my parents, 'I'm not going back.' I would have transferred to another college before I went back to Wellesley. They said I could drop out if I got a job and took some college courses. So I enrolled in night classes at The New School in New York and got a job at *The New Yorker*."

The first issue of *The New Yorker* was dated February 21, 1925 (the year my mother was born). Her father had read the magazine from its inception, and she followed suit, as did I. There has never been a time when *The New Yorker* wasn't read regularly by someone in our family.

"I'd had jobs before," my mother later reminisced. "The summer I was fifteen, I got work papers and worked as a salesgirl at Saks 34th Street. And there were other jobs after that. At *The New Yorker*, I was what they called an office girl. The hours were 9:45 to 5:45, five days a week. I typed. I proofread. I ran errands. I called press agents to find out what was playing for the 'Goings on Around Town' section in the magazine. I opened mail and sent back unsolicited manuscripts with rejection letters. *The New Yorker* only considered manuscripts that came in from agents or writers the editors already knew. I was instructed to return all other submissions with a 'we regret to tell you' letter. No one at *The New Yorker* ever read them. I covered for the receptionist when she went out to lunch. The hardest thing I did was work the switchboard. There were about a hundred people in the office. The switchboard operator had to answer the phone for all of them and put the right plug in the right socket to put the call through. But eventually, it became second nature to me."

Working at *The New Yorker*, my mother interacted with literary luminaries like E.B. White, Katherine White, Harold Ross, Lillian Ross, and William Shawn. "Brendan Gill, who was one of the *New Yorker* writers, was very nice to me," she remembered. "So was Hamilton Basso, who reviewed books for the magazine. Hamilton used to give me books to take home, which I almost always read. They paid me $35 a week, $29.55 after deductions. And I loved it. I would have taken the job for nothing."

Then my mother met my father.

There was no keeper of history on my father's side of the family. He was an only child and, unlike my mother, had little interest in genealogy. His knowledge of ancestry dated back no further than his grandparents.

He was born on November 11, 1917 and named Simon Jaskow Hauser. His paternal grandfather (also named Simon Hauser) was born in Germany, immigrated to the United States, married a woman named Esther Bergstrasser, and worked in a wholesale meat market in New Jersey. Simon and Esther had eight children, the fourth of whom (Isaac, known as Ike) was my father's father. Ike carried on in the family trade as a butcher in Newark.

Solomon Jaskowitz, my father's maternal grandfather, was born in what's now the Czech Republic and moved to New York where he married Sophia Friedman and worked as a hatter. Solomon and Sophia had seven children, the fourth of whom was my father's mother (Rose).

I don't recall meeting any of Ike's seven siblings. I knew one of Rose's sisters (Flossie) and two of her brothers (Sam and Louis).

Sam was an iconic figure in my father's eyes. He was born in 1873 and dropped out of school at an early age to help support the family. His first job paid twenty cents a day. He swept floors and did other menial chores at a firm that bought and sold diamonds. His parents told him that he could keep the twenty cents (paid in pennies) that he earned on that first day of work. He put them in a safe place and kept them for decades.

Sam moved up the ladder at the firm to become a salesman. In 1905, he changed his name from Jaskowitz to Jaskow. Eventually, he founded a company of his own that bought and sold diamonds. He became wealthy and bought a house on St. Nicholas Avenue in Harlem that he, his mother, and his unmarried sisters lived in.

Rose idolized Sam, doted on my father, and looked down on her husband. When my father was a year old, she left Ike and took my father to live with her at Sam's home on St. Nicholas Avenue. A year later, she returned to Ike in New Jersey.

Sam never married. Eventually, he moved to an apartment on Park Avenue in Manhattan and bought a summer home on Lake Mahopac, fifty miles north of the city. The house (called "Rockledge") stood on a large flat rock outcropping and had been built facing the lake. Well-kept gardens swept across the undulating grounds. An inscription chiseled into the mantel above the fireplace read, "A world of care shut out. A world of love shut in." Sam spent hours each week during the summer months fishing at the edge of the lake. Any family member was welcome to stay at Rockledge when the house was open.

Sam also offered to pay for college (and in my father's case, law school as well) for any of his nephews who sought higher education. His generosity allowed my father to become the first member of his family to go to college. Nieces weren't included in the offer.

When I was twelve years old, Sam told me his origin story. Then he gave me the twenty pennies. Years later, I gave one to my brother. I still have the others.

My father enrolled in college at Columbia in September 1935. He did well academically, was president of his college fraternity, and made friends who he remained close with throughout his life. After college, he went to law school at Columbia. Then he was hired as an associate by Nordlinger Riegelman & Cooper—the law firm that my grandfather had founded.

One day, my mother (who was eighteen years old and working at *The New Yorker*) came to the office to have lunch with her father. He introduced her to the recently hired lawyer. That afternoon, my father asked his boss, "Do you think your daughter would go out with me for dinner?"

My grandfather, with characteristic candor, replied, "I don't know. Ask her."

My grandparents liked Si (as he was known). They hadn't liked Buddy. My grandfather tended to have a laissez faire attitude toward those things. My grandmother encouraged the new relationship.

And Buddy was in the Army.

My father was good-looking, sophisticated, and smart. He and my mother began dating. He proposed marriage. She was nineteen years old. He was twenty-seven. Her vision for the future was limited by the expectations of that era. Women were supposed to get married, have children, and rely on their husband for support. And as my mother later explained, "I wanted to leave home and be my own boss. I didn't want my mother telling me what to do anymore."

Their engagement was announced in the *New York Times* on March 22, 1945. Brendan Gill cut the announcement with my mother's photograph out of the newspaper and posted it on a bulletin board at *The New Yorker*. She and my father were married in a non-denominational ceremony at my grandparents' home on June 24, 1945.

A professional photographer captured the scene in two dozen black-and-white photographs. The photos begin with my father knotting his tie in a mirror above the dresser in my mother's bedroom. Then my mother is shown powdering her face in front of the same mirror. My grandmother helps my mother put on her bridal veil. My mother and father pose together in front of the fireplace in the living room where the ceremony will be held. Other family members are pictured with them. There's the ceremony. The first kiss after marriage. A champagne toast. Cutting the wedding cake. Dancing. Finally, the happy couple is shown departing for a lifetime of marital bliss.

The perfect tableau.

Except, years later, my mother would remember asking herself that night, "Why am I marrying this man when I love Buddy?"

Chapter II

"I was so young when I got married," my mother said late in life. "In some ways, I was mature for my age. But I'd never been on my own. I'd never had to balance a budget or do all the other things you do when you have your own home."

And she'd never been responsible for another person who was totally dependent on her for survival and demanded attention every minute of every day except when he was asleep.

Then I was born.

I can't write about my mother without writing about myself. There came a time when I understood that she had an identity beyond being my mother. But for years, I viewed her largely through the prism of my own life.

I was a wedding night accident. My mother told me that, once the surprise of being pregnant wore off, she looked forward to my arrival. She and my father had planned to have children. This simply accelerated the process. Shortly before her twentieth birthday, she quit her job at *The New Yorker*. Two months later, I was born.

After my parents were married, they moved into a one-bedroom apartment on the west side of Manhattan. When I was two, we moved to a two-bedroom apartment in New Rochelle just north of New York City in suburban Westchester.

I remember bits and pieces about the New Rochelle apartment. It was in one of four six-story buildings known as Locust Court that ringed a small park. I remember one glorious Christmas morning being brought into the living room by my mother and seeing my father sitting on the floor next to a Lionel electric train that was chugging around a circular track. There was a big smile on his face. He pushed a lever on the transformer and a whistle sounded.

I also have a vivid memory of a tragedy, although I didn't understand that it was a tragedy at the time.

One night when I was three years old, I was awakened by frantic activity outside my bedroom door. My mother was visibly upset. My father was helping her put a coat over her nightgown (which was sea green). That's all I remember from that night. I went back to sleep. In the morning, my parents were gone. It was the first time I'd woken up without one of them there.

My mother had suffered a miscarriage. Much later, I learned that she'd suffered two previous miscarriages. But those had occurred early in pregnancy. This one came late. In today's world, the baby might have been saved. My father took my mother to the hospital and stayed with her overnight. My grandparents were at our apartment for dinner when it happened. My grandfather went to the hospital with my parents and then back into the city.

My grandmother made breakfast for me. She took a bowl and poured some cereal into it. Then she went to the refrigerator for milk and put a piece of bread in the toaster. When breakfast was ready, she handed me a spoon that was too big to fit in my mouth and I showed her the right spoon. I remember feeling secure that morning. I knew that, regardless of where my mother and father were, everything would be all right because Grandma Elise was there.

It would be decades before I understood the emotional impact that three miscarriages had on my mother.

When I was four, my brother Jim was born.

In 1952, we moved to a house in Larchmont—a suburban community eighteen miles northeast of Manhattan. That same year, the last of my siblings—my sister Lise—was born.

I assume there was a time when I called my parents Mommy and Daddy. But as far back as I can remember, I called them Mom and Dad.

Our new home was on a quiet street called Eton Road. Jim, Lise, and I had separate bedrooms. Mine overlooked a portion of the backyard that, in my imagination, was shaped like the playing field at Yankee Stadium.

My parents now had three young children. That demanded a huge amount of Mom's time. She and my father also had an active social life and spent most Friday and Saturday nights with friends who were virtually all Jewish (as their own parents' social circles had been). That was the world in the 1950s.

My father commuted to the city by train five days a week and worked at the firm on legal matters ranging from general litigation and corporate filings to trusts and estates. Eventually, he rose from being one of four associates in the office to one of five partners.

He had a passion for gardening. From early spring through mid-autumn, our yard was a tapestry of flowers with a vegetable garden thrown into the mix. Mom missed the energy of the city, its museums, theater, and all the other things New York has to offer. But Larchmont was a nice place to live.

I walked to Murray Avenue Elementary School with a next-door neighbor who was in the same class that I was. If it was raining, one of our mothers drove us.

Mom took me to the library for books, as her mother had done for her when she was a child. My father read to me at night when he put me to bed.

Larchmont wasn't formally segregated. But there were no Negro (the accepted term at that time) teachers or students at Murray Avenue. In looking at the photos in my high school yearbook, I see eight Black students in my graduating class of 350. And no Black teachers.

There came a time when a local chapter of the NAACP asked residents of Eton Road to sign a statement pledging that, if they sold their home, they would be willing to sell to a Negro family and that they wouldn't object if a neighbor's home was sold to a Negro family. My parents were the only homeowners on the block who signed the pledge.

Parents work together to raise children. But years later, Mom told me, "I don't remember Si and I discussing parenting often. That sort of discussion was less common in our era than it is now."

I learned how to swim and ride a bike. I played Monopoly, Scrabble, checkers, chess, and a board game called All-Star Baseball.

My father was only casually interested in sports; my mother, not at all. I loved sports, both as a participant and a fan. I lived and died with the New York Yankees. Mickey Mantle was in my pantheon of gods.

Another memory that I have of childhood is of Mom saying to Dad (as she often did), "Hurry up, Si. We'll be late." Later in life, I realized that my father was always on time. Left to her own devices, Mom was always early.

And there are scars. I was a fat kid. Later, I slimmed down.

I'm six-feet-three-inches tall (taller than anyone ever in our family). But I was overweight at an age when self-image is formed. Each year in elementary school, the students were weighed and measured for height. For reasons that still escape me, my fifth-grade teacher decided to write how tall everyone in the class was and how much we weighed on a chart that she hung on a wall in the back of the room. That way, if anyone forgot who the fattest kid in the class was, they could check out the chart.

One day when I was in sixth grade, I rode my bike into Larchmont village to buy a comic book. A girl I had a crush on (my first crush) was in the store. I said hello and she cheerfully replied that she had written a poem for me.

"Would you like to hear it?"

With great anticipation, I answered in the affirmative. She gathered her thoughts and recited, "Ho ho, you big fatso."

I'm sure she doesn't remember that moment. Almost seventy years later, I do.

Mom's side of the family was more involved with our lives than Dad's was. Christmas, birthdays, and other occasions were celebrated at my grandparents' apartment.

My grandfather was a shade over five feet ten inches tall, had a big pot belly, and weighed thirty pounds more than he should have. There was an old balance scale in the bathroom that he weighed himself on every morning. But he never lost weight. He shaved with a straight razor and carried a gold Hamilton pocket watch on a chain attached at one end to a belt loop and tucked into a vest or pants pocket at the other. He had the delightful custom of giving out presents on his own birthday. I got more presents on my birthday than I did on his.

But as a child, I looked forward to his birthday for obvious reasons.

On occasion, I slept over at my grandparents' apartment on Saturday night. When I did, my grandfather took me down to the subway on Sunday morning. We'd get on the first train that came into the station and ride it till the end of the line. I'd stand in front and look out the window at the signal lights and tracks ahead while he read the *New York Times*.

My grandmother took me on my first trip (to Washington D.C.), my first Broadway play (*Peter Pan*), and my first night baseball game (it wasn't because she liked night baseball). She also stood in line with me for ninety minutes in sub-freezing temperature so I could see the Mona Lisa when it was on display at the Metropolitan Museum of Art.

Mom's brother (Ed) was only twelve years older than me. I looked up to him the way that young boys look up to an uncle who takes them to baseball games and plays catch with them in the backyard.

Mom's sister (Ruth) was the polar opposite of my mother. She struggled in school, was physically ungainly, and tended to complain. When I was eleven, Ruth got engaged to a man named Gerry Wexelman who installed air conditioners for a living, and my grandmother took the subway to Brooklyn to have lunch with her future son-in-law's mother.

"My boy, Gerry, he's a good boy," Mrs. Wexelman told my grandmother. "He's never been in jail."

Ruth and Gerry had a daughter. When she was two, Gerry left. Ruth never heard from him again. Ten years later, she remarried and tried to track Gerry down as part of an adoption proceeding but couldn't locate him.

I never knew my father's father. He died before I was born. Rose (my father's mother) had a generally sour demeanor. When my parents got engaged, Rosie (as she was known) told

Mom, "Don't get a double bed. If you do and you have a cold, you'll give it to Si." Early in my parents' marriage, my father lost ten pounds after a bout with dysentery. When Rosie saw him, she shouted at my mother, "What have you done to my son?"

Years later, Mom told me, "Buddy had a mother named Rose who liked me. And before Buddy, I went out with a boy named Ben Heller who had a mother named Rose who liked me. I wound up with the worst of the Roses."

∼

When I was ten, Mom and Dad decided that I should go to sleepaway camp. That seemed like a palatable idea until I realized I'd be leaving home for the first time and spending eight weeks at a place called Camp Winnebago in Fayette, Maine.

Campers from the New York City metropolitan area traveled to Winnebago overnight by train. On the evening I left, I held back the tears until I was onboard and started crying as the train pulled out of the station. Several days later, I got a letter from Mom (which I still have in a scrapbook): "Dear Tom, I was never so proud of anyone as I was of you last night when you went off so bravely. Of course it felt strange for you to be leaving us for the first time, but there has to be a first time for everything. And knowing what a truly fine and wonderful boy you are, you will make a happy adventure out of your summer."

I was horribly homesick for the first week and then slowly adjusted. Three more summers at Camp Winnebago followed.

Meanwhile, students from Murray Avenue and three other public elementary schools in the area fed into Mamaroneck Junior High School. Like every other kid in seventh grade, I was dealing with the stirrings of puberty. I was socially awkward (particularly with girls) and still overweight.

So, of course, my parents sent me to dancing school.

Dancing school was a system of torture designed with young adolescents like me in mind. We were taught to lindy, foxtrot, waltz, and cha-cha. Mr. and Mrs. Barry were the instructors. At the start of each session, they'd demonstrate a particular dance step. Then each boy would ask a girl to dance. I'd lumber around the floor to a recording of whatever top-40 hit was playing, after which the Barrys would offer a few words of instruction and the rite of asking another girl to dance began.

One evening, I asked a girl to dance. All of us have done cruel things in our lives that we now regret. So, I won't mention her name. I'll call her "X."

In violation of all protocol, X refused my invitation to dance for the stated reason that I was "ooky." Instead of letting the matter drop, Mr. Barry turned off the record player, made me stand in the center of the room next to X, and delivered a lecture on etiquette. His words, which I remember to this day, were, "Now, boys and girls, even if Tommy Hauser [he called me Tommy] were ooky—and mind you, I'm not saying that he is —but even if Tommy Hauser were ooky, the polite thing for X to do would be to dance with him. It wouldn't kill X to dance one dance with someone she doesn't like."

Then the real "real world" intervened.

My father was a gentle man. There was no ill will in his character. I have memories of hiking and fishing with him when I was a boy and building a barbeque pit made of stones in the backyard. He was emotionally distant and steered clear of difficult subjects. I don't remember his ever talking about feelings. He never counseled me about the rudiments of sex.

When I was thirteen, a pall (although I didn't recognize it as such) hung over our home. Then, one afternoon, I came home from school. Dad always got home from work around six thirty. It was three thirty and he was lying on the bed.

I asked if he was sick.

"I don't know," he said.

"Can I get you anything?"

"Just sit here with me."

He didn't want to talk. He just lay there. I sat with him for a while. Then I heard the front door open. Mom was home. I met her just inside the door.

"Dad's home."

"Where?"

"In the bedroom. I think he's sick."

Mom rushed into the bedroom with an urgency that I still remember. She knew what I didn't. My father had been sliding toward a breakdown.

Psychosis is a loss of contact with reality. Someone suffering from psychosis has trouble distinguishing between what's real and what isn't. Neurosis manifests itself as depression.

My father was severely depressed. And his condition had worsened to the point where he could no longer function. He stopped going to the office. Some days, he wouldn't have been able to get there on his own if he'd tried. He was incapable of coping with life's routines and challenges.

One day, Mom asked him to make the bed.

"I can't," he said.

Depression was poorly understood and rarely talked about decades ago. My father was hospitalized and subjected to electroshock therapy twelve times. Electroshock therapy in 1959 was a crude technique that induced seizures by applying voltage to a patient's head to "shake up the brain." Even in its more sophisticated form, it's rarely used today because of cognitive side effects like memory loss and the existence of more effective treatments.

I remember one sit-down with Mom in the months after I

came home from school and found my father lying on the bed. She told me that Dad wasn't well and we'd all have to pull together and he needed our love and support. I distanced myself emotionally from his illness. In my mind, it was happening to someone else, not me. I didn't understand that, while my father was the one suffering the most, it was happening to all of us.

Years later, I tried to imagine the deep dark pit that my father had been in and the fear he must have felt. He would get better and then relapse. Better and relapse. He was incapacitated on and off for eight years. Decades later when I went into therapy myself, one of the first things my therapist said to me was, "You put a lot of varnish over your feelings in those early years."

It was also a hard time for my mother. She was almost solely responsible for three children in addition to caring for my father. Some wives would have reached a point where they took the children and left. But that's not who she was.

Our family had always been financially comfortable. But as Dad's illness dragged on, money became an issue. My mother returned to the workforce as a receptionist and administrator in a doctor's office. I mowed lawns, raked leaves, shoveled snow, babysat, and took other odd jobs.

The 1960 presidential election was a bonding experience for Mom and me. Both of us were captivated by John Kennedy (who was the same age as my father).

I was a good student. I wasn't rebellious. For the most part, I followed rules in and out of the home. I shoplifted twice, didn't get caught, didn't like the feeling, and never did it again.

I did get caught in a lie in what might be called "the Sara

Lee banana cake incident." One evening before dinner, I was hungry. So, I took an already-opened Sara Lee banana cake out of the refrigerator, removed the wax paper from inside the box, and sliced off a piece of cake. Minutes later . . .

"Why did you eat cake just now?" Mom demanded. There was irritation in her voice. "We're having dinner in twenty minutes."

I don't remember why I lied. But I did.

"I didn't eat cake."

"Yes, you did."

"No, I didn't."

My mother was getting angry now. No one likes to be lied to by their children no matter how inconsequential the lie might be.

"I don't mind that you ate some cake. I mind it a lot that you're lying to me. And before you dig yourself in deeper . . ."

Then Mom pointed to the piece of wax paper from inside the box that I'd inadvertently left on the kitchen counter. That seemed like a good time to confess that, yes, I'd eaten a piece of cake.

Meanwhile, the rituals of adolescence continued. The day I turned sixteen, Mom drove me to the County Clerk's office in White Plains so I could get my learner's permit. Later that afternoon, she gave me my first driving lesson in an empty parking lot. There was one bush in the center of the lot, and I hit it. But she was a good teacher. When the time came, I passed my road test on the first try.

In autumn of my senior year of high school, some friends and I decided to pick the winners of college football games and take bets from other students at lunchtime in the cafeteria. In other words, we were bookies. We made a few dollars. Then we started filling out college applications that, among other questions, asked, "Have you ever been suspended from school? If so, state the reason why." Discretion being the better part of valor, our bookie days came to an end.

I was still socially awkward and didn't date. Mom tried to prod me into dating (gently, I'm sure she thought). How do you explain to someone who was pursued all through her own high school years that you'd like to go out with girls but can't?

The first date I had was for the senior prom. One evening, I telephoned an equally shy girl whom I actually liked.

"Would you like to go to the senior prom with me?"

"Let me ask my father," she said.

There was a wait that I'm sure wasn't as long as it seemed. Then she came back on the line.

"Yes."

And there's another moment that I remember particularly well. I'd applied to four colleges—Columbia, Harvard, Johns Hopkins, and Syracuse. Harvard was my first choice. I hadn't made up my mind as to whether I preferred Columbia or Johns Hopkins but was leaning toward Columbia.

Ivy League colleges sent out acceptance and rejection letters by mail in those days. The mail was reliable. The letters were timed to arrive on the same day. And applicants knew when that day would be.

I was at home, waiting with Mom, when the mailman (they weren't called "mail carriers" in 1963) arrived. There were two envelopes addressed to me. One from Columbia and one from Harvard.

I opened the envelope from Harvard first.

"Dear Mr. Hauser, We regret to inform you . . ."

I hadn't expected to get into Harvard. And the look on my face told my mother that I hadn't.

Then I opened the letter from Columbia.

"Dear Mr. Hauser, It is my pleasure to inform you that . . ."

An acceptance letter from Johns Hopkins came in the mail

the next day. But by then, I'd made up my mind that I was going to Columbia.

~

I pieced together several scholarships that covered most of my tuition at Columbia and lived in the dorms during my undergraduate years.

Given my interest in sports, it was just a matter of time before I got involved with WKCR (the student-run radio station). I called play-by-play for some Columbia basketball games. But my most notable contribution to WKCR was creating and hosting a weekly radio show called *Personalities in Sports*.

Each week, I'd take a bulky old reel-to-reel tape recorder into the field and interview the biggest names I could get. Joe Namath . . . Pete Rozelle . . . Willis Reed . . . I reached nirvana one afternoon when I found myself in the New York Yankees dugout just prior to a doubleheader as the Yankees readied to clinch their fourteenth pennant in sixteen years. Tom Tresh gave me my first interview; Whitey Ford, my second. Then Mickey Mantle came into the dugout.

With great anticipation, I approached my boyhood idol.

"Mr. Mantle. My name is Tom Hauser, and I wonder if I could interview you for WKCR."

"Fuck."

That was all he said. Not even "fuck you." Just "fuck" (which I assumed meant "no," since he then turned and walked away).

I came into my own at Columbia. In a world divided into kids who were cool and kids who were nerds, I'd always been a nerd. At Columbia, there were niches where everyone could feel comfortable and valued. At the close of my junior year, I was elected senior class president (which seemed like a big deal at the time). The margin of victory was one vote.

During my Columbia years, I also came to the realization that women (some women, at least) thought I was good-looking with a certain level of intelligence and charm. That made the world a sunnier place.

I'd had my first kiss the summer after I graduated from high school (a late age even in that sheltered era). The following summer while working as a day-camp counselor, I'd met the first girl I ever really liked who went out with me. We went to a movie and an amusement park, after which she dumped me for the baseball instructor. At age twenty (also an advanced age) I had my first sexual experience. That led to a much-too-long period when I slept with more women than I should have (which I now regret).

Meanwhile, all of this was happening against the backdrop of the Sixties.

John Kennedy's assassination in November of my freshman year was a shattering experience for me. He'd been my hero and, in some ways, a substitute father figure. That was followed by cataclysmic shifts in American life marked by the Civil Rights Movement, opposition to the war in Vietnam, and a new, more powerful youth culture.

My father's illness dragged on. Over the years, he'd been granted several leaves of absence from work. While I was in college, that tolerance came to an end. My grandfather had been the law firm's guiding light from its inception. Now one of his partners had seized the reins of power.

During my senior year of college, my father was hospitalized again, this time for six months. My mother visited him twice a week. I was allowed to visit once during the time that he was an in-patient Eventually, he was permitted to come home on weekends (Friday afternoon to Sunday night). As his release from the hospital neared, my grandfather's partner told my mother, "When Si gets out, I think he should take a long rest from work and find a less pressured job. That's not negotiable," he added.

In 1967, at age fifty, Dad took a job with the Law Department for the City of New York. Several years later, he began working for an attorney who had an already-established private practice. Miraculously—I don't use that word often—he never relapsed again.

Years later, Dad told me, "I don't know why I got sick, and I don't know why I got well. It just happened."

Going to law school after college was a natural next step for me. Columbia offered me a full-tuition scholarship, and I lived with my grandparents during the first year of law school. Then, with my father working again, I got an apartment with two roommates several blocks from the Columbia campus.

Law school taught me to think analytically in a way that I hadn't thought before. At the start of my final year, I started looking at jobs and decided it would be a good idea to clerk for a federal district court judge.

The United States district courts are trial courts with jurisdiction over civil and criminal cases. Each judge has two law clerks who do research and write legal memoranda for a year or two before moving on to other jobs. It's a good way for newly minted law school graduates to learn about litigation and the federal courts.

In December 1969, I was granted an interview with Thomas F. Croake, John Kennedy's first judicial appointee in the Southern District of New York (the court with jurisdiction over federal cases in Manhattan, the Bronx, and six counties to the north). We talked for a while in the judge's chambers. Then . . . "You'll do," the judge said.

Judge Croake wasn't a scholar. But he was a marvelous

teacher. Each day at work was marked by an explanation as to why a brief submitted by a lawyer should have been drafted differently or how an attorney could have improved his court-room presentation to better serve a client.

One day, the judge told me, "There's a young assistant United States Attorney who's making an opening statement this afternoon in a criminal case in Judge Bryan's courtroom. You ought to sit in to see how it's done."

The assistant United States Attorney was 26-year-old Rudy Giuliani.

I clerked for Judge Croake for a year before transitioning to a job as a litigator at a large Wall Street law firm. Before starting on Wall Street, I took three months off and drove cross country.

I'm well-traveled now. Prior to 1971, outside of my grand-mother taking me to Washington D.C. when I was ten, I'd never been out of the northeast. The cross-country trip was my first real travel experience.

I bought a used car. There were times when I stayed with people I knew. Otherwise, I camped out or stayed in cheap motels. Two friends flew out and joined me at different times during the journey. For much of the trip, I was alone.

I visited cities and small towns and spent several days at a commune in Wolf Creek, Oregon. I drove through cornfields in Iowa, wheat in Nebraska, and potatoes in Idaho. I saw Elvis Presley perform live in Las Vegas, retraced the route that John Kennedy traveled in Dallas on November 22, 1963, and walked the streets of Selma at a time when the "N-word" was commonly used. The Grand Canyon filled me with awe.

I saw America. That was the goal. Then I settled into a new life as a lawyer at Cravath Swaine & Moore.

Cravath can trace its lineage to 1819. In the early-1970s, it had forty partners and 140 associates (it now has roughly three times that number) and occupied the fifty-sixth through fifty-eighth floors in a sixty-story skyscraper two blocks north of Wall Street. I'd been offered a job there during my final year of law school, and the firm held the offer open until my clerkship ended.

Cravath was considered by many to be the best law firm in the country. That's a subjective judgment. Mom took pride in the fact that I was there. The firm's corporate and litigation departments were its engines of power. There was one woman partner. My office, which I shared with an older associate, looked out over the Statue of Liberty.

During my first year, I worked almost exclusively on First Amendment matters. Most of my time was spent defending CBS, *Time Magazine*, and other clients against libel suits. Then the rotation process kicked in, and I was assigned to an antitrust case that had been brought against Westinghouse (our client) and General Electric. Litigation involving securities law and other corporate-oriented matters followed.

There was little actual trial work. Most cases were settled after lengthy discovery proceedings. The few cases that reached trial were tried by a partner. Then one of the partners circulated a memorandum asking if anyone was interested in handling a criminal case that he thought the firm should accept on a pro bono basis. A 20-year-old black man had been indicted for the attempted murder of two policeman. The evidence, the partner believed, strongly suggested that he was innocent.

I wanted to put what I'd learned during my clerkship into practice. I volunteered and tried the case in front of a jury. Then I sat with my heart pounding as the jurors returned to the courtroom after their deliberations.

"What is your verdict?" the judge asked.

"Not guilty," the foreman said.

Cravath had an up-or-out policy. After seven or eight years, each associate was considered for partnership. The chosen few had security for life. Those who were passed over had to find new jobs (but with a Cravath pedigree to help them).

I didn't wait for a decision on my future. After five years, I was ready to move on. There were plusses to working at Cravath. I was surrounded by smart people. The work could be intellectually challenging. It paid well. But I was getting bored. It didn't help that I was spending long hours on a case that involved the issue of whether the cost of funds used during construction had been properly capitalized as an item of other income on the consolidated balance sheet of the Detroit Edison Company. I realized that, even though $88 million was involved, I didn't care.

So, I started looking at other jobs. Law firms with a different type of practice, the U.S. Attorney's Office and American Civil Liberties Union, philanthropic foundations. And I realized that I didn't want to practice law anymore.

That was a problem. I was thirty-one years old.

I'd always liked writing—term papers in school, memoranda for Judge Croake, legal briefs, whatever. And I was intrigued by the idea that, a hundred years from now, someone might come across a book I'd written and spend a few hours with it. I decided to devote a year to writing to learn if I enjoyed the lifestyle and could support myself doing it.

I left Cravath on April 15, 1977, at 6:05 PM (give or take a few seconds). Looking back on the years that I devoted to the law, it was a satisfying part of my life. I learned a new level of professionalism and acquired skills that have served me well. But leaving the law to write was probably the best decision I've made in my life.

I left Cravath with a project in hand. When I was clerking for Judge Croake, I'd met a woman named Terry Simon. Three years later, in September 1973, Terry was in Chile visiting a husband and wife named Charles and Joyce Horman (American nationals living in Santiago) when a military coup overthrew the freely elected government of Chilean president Salvador Allende. Thousands of people were brutally murdered by the ruling Junta in the reign of terror that followed. Charles was one of them.

In the months after Charles's death, his parents came to question whether United States government officials in Chile (who, a Congressional investigation later revealed, were complicit in planning the coup) were covering up facts surrounding Charles's murder. Or worse, that one or more of these officials might have had foreknowledge of, or even ordered, Charles's execution. Terry asked if I'd be willing to meet with Charles's parents to discuss what legal options might be available to them in their pursuit of the truth.

I met with Ed and Elizabeth Horman in late 1973. Three years later, when I began to consider writing as a career, Charles's story came to mind. It had a dramatic narrative arc. Important issues were unresolved. I asked the Hormans if they'd be willing to cooperate with me if I wrote a book. They encouraged it.

I submitted a proposal to a dozen publishing houses. There was one offer—a $6,500 advance against royalties from Harcourt Brace Jovanovich—which I accepted.

My mother was unhappy when I told her I was leaving Cravath to write. She was afraid that I was throwing away my future.

"Don't worry," I told her. "If writing doesn't work out, I can go back to law."

The book was published in 1978 under the title *The Execution of Charles Horman*. The dedication read, "To my mother and father, who have always stood by me."

The book made waves. A commentary in the *New York*

Times called it "devastating." The *Los Angeles Times* proclaimed, "Hauser's reconstruction of the events leading up to Horman's death reads like the scenario of a Hitchcock thriller. One does not have to have known Charles Horman or his wife and family to be saddened and outraged by this book." I was interviewed by Tom Brokaw on *The Today Show*. Then Universal Studios purchased motion picture rights to the book. That led to an Academy-Award-winning film titled *Missing* starring Jack Lemmon and Sissy Spacek that was directed by Costa-Gavras.

Shortly before the film opened, Universal rented a small screening room and told me that I could invite any thirty people I wanted to a private viewing. When the screening ended, Mom turned to me and said, "I can't believe it. It's a real movie."

"Of course, it's a real movie."

"I know you said it would be a movie. But I thought it would be a documentary or something like that. This is a real movie."

Then things got complicated. Three United States Government officials who'd been in Chile at the time of the coup filed a libel suit against Harcourt, Avon (which had published the book in paperback), Costa-Gavras, Universal, and myself. Next, despite the unfounded nature of the lawsuit, Harcourt and Avon took the book out of print on the theory that, if a court were to rule against them, taking it out of print would lessen any court-awarded damages. *New York Times* columnist Anthony Lewis wrote an Op Ed piece calling the publishers' conduct "craven" and saying that *Missing* was "an important book, at the very core of what the First Amendment is supposed to protect." I asked the publishers to revert rights so I could find another publisher, and they refused. So, I sued them. I had already counterclaimed against the libel plaintiffs.

Ultimately, the libel suit was dismissed. But the three government officials who'd sued still had my counterclaim to deal with. The end result was that they signed a consent order agreeing that they would never again sue any future publisher of the book; *Missing* was republished; and I walked away from the various pieces of litigation with a settlement totaling several hundred thousand dollars.

Decades later, there was a coda to the proceedings. In 2014, a Chilean court ruled after an extensive investigation that Ray Davis (head of the United States Military Group in Chile at the time of the coup and one of the libel plaintiffs) had, in fact, played a role in Charles Horman's murder. More specifically, the court found conclusive evidence that Davis had provided the Chilean military with information that led to Charles's arrest and execution and also the death of another American named Frank Teruggi.

While all of this was going on, I kept writing. My second book focused on a white policeman who was indicted and tried for murder after shooting a ten-year-old Black boy in the back. I did my best to humanize both sides of the story. After the book was published, I received letters of commendation from both the president of the New York City Patrolmen's Benevolent Association and the NAACP.

Then I tried my hand at fiction, writing a love story titled *Ashworth & Palmer* that was set in a large Wall Street law firm not unlike Cravath. The firm librarian bought three copies for the Cravath law library (its first novel ever). On hearing the news, John R. Hupper (head of the firm's litigation department) marched into the library, removed all three copies from the shelves, and threw them out.

I liked writing fiction. A good novel requires research but the most interesting part of working on a novel is the actual writing. That's when the characters come alive for me. They're always running through my mind and doing things I hadn't planned for them. When I'm working on a novel, regardless of where I am, I have a pen and paper with me to take notes. I sleep with a pen and pad by my bed.

Three murder mysteries and a spy story set in the mountains of Nepal followed. Mom got a kick out of it when *The New Yorker* reviewed one of the murder mysteries (*The Beethoven Conspiracy*) and called it "first class entertainment."

After that, I returned to non-fiction, co-authoring the first of what would be three values-oriented books with Frank Macchiarola (a lifelong friend and mentor), who had a distinguished career as Chancellor of the New York City School system, Dean of Cardozo Law School, and President of St. Francis College. While working with Frank, I started research on another non-fiction book—*The Black Lights: Inside the World of Professional Boxing*. I didn't know it then, but boxing would change my life.

Meanwhile, the success of *Missing* led to my being asked to co-author a book about Chernobyl with Dr. Robert Gale (the bone marrow transplant specialist brought to the Soviet Union by Mikhail Gorbachev to treat firemen who'd been sickened by radiation in the aftermath of the nuclear reactor explosion). I'd heard that Dr. Gale was brilliant but difficult to work with. I found him to be a wonderful collaborator. When the book was done, I mentioned the warning I'd been given and he told me, "There might be some validity to it. I don't suffer fools gladly. But you're not a fool."

And there was another benefit that came with the Chernobyl book. It was made into a film starring Jason Robards and Jon Voight. That led to a Saturday night conversation when I was sound asleep and the telephone rang around 1:00 a.m. It was Voight, who wanted to talk about character motivation. My initial thought was, "This is fantastic. Jon Voight! *Midnight*

Cowboy, Deliverance, Coming Home (for which Voight had previously won Best Actor honors at the Academy Awards)."

But on this particular call, Voight's thoughts were disjointed. He rambled. The conversation went on. And on. There came a point when it occurred to me that, unless I extricated myself, I might be on the phone until dawn. So, I told him that it was an honor to talk with him but it was late. Voight said he'd call back in a day or two, and I never heard from him again.

While I was exploring new frontiers, my mother's life had settled into a routine. Her three children were out of the home. Dad was working again. Rosie (his mother) died in 1970 but he took her passing in stride.

Mom had always been interested in economics. In the early 1970s, she began taking a weekly course in investing to better manage her own finances. Around that time, she went to a Fieldston alumni reunion where one of her classmates who'd founded a successful investment firm offered her a job as a customer representative.

"I discussed it with Si," Mom said years later. "He'd finally stabilized. Taking the job would have meant another change when things were just getting back to normal and I was ambivalent about commuting to the city five days a week, so I turned it down."

In 1976, my grandfather died. It was the first death in the family that cut deep for me. He was bedridden for the last two months of his life but cognitively sharp. I visited him every Saturday as the end neared.

"I'm worried," my grandfather told me the last time I saw him. "I woke up during the night and couldn't go back to sleep, so I played *Die Walkure* through in my mind."

Die Walkure was his favorite opera. Performed in its entirety, it lasts well over four hours. He'd seen it dozens of times.

"What's worrying you?"

"I looked at the clock when I started and then when I finished. It took twenty minutes less than it should have. I think I left something out."

"Did you perform it with or without intermissions?"

"I took that into account."

"Maybe you performed it at a slightly faster pace than Wagner intended."

"You might be right."

The day my grandfather died, we gathered as a family at my grandparents' apartment. My mother was crying.

"Death sucks," she said.

Several months later, my grandmother moved to a smaller apartment. I'd always liked a small black-and-white photo of Central Park in the snow that had been shot from their bedroom window at The Majestic in the 1930s and hung on a wall in their apartment. I asked my grandmother if I could have it, but she wanted to keep it (which was fine). When she unpacked after the move and set up her new home, she couldn't find the photo and asked me to give it back.

"I don't have it."

"Yes, you do."

That was atypical of our relationship. I'd never lied to her, and she'd never thought of me as lying. But for whatever reason, she didn't believe me. It bothered both of us.

Fast-forward to 1983. I was at my grandmother's apartment for dinner. We were talking about family, which we often did. She loved to reminisce about her brothers (Richard and Lyman) and Lyman's wife (Polly). After dinner, we decided to look at old photographs.

"There's a box I haven't looked at in years," my grandmother told me. "It's on the top shelf in the hallway closet."

I took the box off the closet shelf, set it down on the coffee table in front of the sofa, and opened it.

There, on top, was the framed photo of Central Park.

"Well I'll be damned," my grandmother said. Then she started laughing and hugged me.

A week later, without warning, my grandmother died.

With my grandmother's death, Mom became the matriarch of the family. She stopped dyeing her hair and let it go gray. She took up bridge at age fifty-nine, was good at it, and regretted not having learned the game earlier so she could have played with her own parents.

I talked on the phone with Mom and Dad several times a week. Once a month or so, I had lunch in the city with my father. On occasion, I took the train to Larchmont for lunch or dinner, to help Dad turn the vegetable garden, whatever. At the end of each year, there was a burst of activity with Thanksgiving, Christmas, and my parents' birthdays.

Mom and Dad were no longer in my daily life (not physically, at least) and hadn't been for years. I'd moved into an apartment on Riverside Drive in Manhattan after graduating from law school and hadn't slept in the home I grew up in for decades.

I certainly didn't have a finger on the pulse of my parents' marriage.

I saw Mom and Dad as having a comfortable life in the suburbs. They'd weathered the storm of my father's illness, faced the normal challenges that come with being married, and had been together for forty-three years.

Then my mother got a letter from Buddy.

Chapter III

G arrison Keillor once wrote, "No one can quite imagine the spark that lit the fire between one's parents."

Or the spark between a parent and someone else. It's an odd position I'm in, writing about that spark. But I'll do my best.

Like most children, I hadn't focused on my parents as people with lives independent of my own. I'd viewed them through the filter of my own experiences. That meant there was a lot I hadn't seen. Or had seen and chose to not think about.

Consider the circumstances. At age nineteen, my mother married a man eight years older than she was. He was charming and smart. Her parents liked him. Counterintuitively, getting married represented a kind of emancipation for her. But Buddy owned a piece of her heart. She and my father moved to the suburbs and had three children. My father became dreadfully ill. Mom's sense of loyalty and responsibility kept her from leaving. She stood by my father. She nursed him, took a job, and carried most of the weight of parenting. The family emerged intact. My father began working productively again.

But Mom was terribly lonely in the marriage. "I don't put all the blame on Si for the shortcomings in our relationship," she later said. "There were two of us in the marriage." That said, my father was emotionally distant and always would be. Once, when Mom felt them drifting apart, she asked if he loved her. Dad's answer was an irritated, "Of course I love you." There was fondness between them but little romantic love. Then, like a life preserver thrown to a drowning woman, a letter from Buddy arrived in the mail.

Buddy was now "Bud" to his friends and known professionally as Bernard D. Nossiter. In 1944, after a year at Dartmouth, he'd been drafted into the Army. Most of his time in the service was spent as a public relations officer in South Carolina. He never saw combat. After the war, he graduated from college, earned a master's degree in economics from Harvard, and took a job working at the copy desk of the *Wall Street Journal*. He was called back to the Army near the end of the Korean War and spent fifteen months stateside, again as a public relations officer. After being discharged, he began work as a general assignment reporter for the *New York World Telegram & Sun*.

In the years that followed, Bud spent twenty-four years with the *Washington Post*, specializing in economics while based in Paris, New Delhi, Washington, and London. Then he joined the *New York Times* as chief of its United Nations Bureau before retiring from journalism to pursue a career as a freelance writer. "The whole point in my mind," he told my mother, "was to enable me to write what I please for whom I please and still live agreeably."

He was a principled journalist and a good one.

Ironically, like my father, Bud had suffered from a crippling depression. In his case, the worst of it had come in 1948. He married two years later and had four sons.

Throughout his adult years, Bud had carried a torch for my mother. After he and my mother reunited (which they did soon after his letter arrived), he told her that he used to walk alone in Central Park and fantasize about meeting her by chance. "I used to imagine running into you," he wrote in a subsequent letter. "We'd stop for a drink, talk pleasantly about kids, grandkids, and the externals of our lives. We'd smile sadly at the end, a discreet signal that we were not entirely indifferent to each other even now."

Not long after *Missing* was released as a film in 1982, a friend of mine who worked at the *New York Times* mentioned my name to Bud during a conversation they were having about Chile. This was shortly after Mom had included a note about the film in a Fieldston alumni update.

"I had to call to tell you this," my friend said. "Bud told me, 'I know who Thomas Hauser is. I've been in love with his mother for forty years.'"

A month before Mom died, we were talking. She was in bed.

"There's a large folder on a shelf in the closet in the den," she told me. "Do you know the one I mean?"

I did.

"Could you bring it to me?"

The folder had a thick, red rubber band around it. I brought it into the bedroom. Mom opened it and took out a stack of pages.

"Those are the letters Bud and I wrote when we started seeing each other again. They're yours. Use them in your book. Do whatever you want. I trust your judgment."

I brought the letters home that afternoon and put them in a closet. Bud had been living in London when he reconnected with my mother. In the months that followed, they wrote more than a hundred letters to each other. There was no email in those days. Each of them kept the letters that the other sent. I didn't read them until after Mom died.

My mother's letters to Bud were handwritten, and her handwriting was remarkably easy to read. Bud typed his letters, which was a blessing since they tended toward the long side and his handwriting was barely legible.

Reading the letters was evocative of the son and daughter in *The Bridges of Madison County* who, after their mother dies, learn of an affair she had when they read her diary. Except by the time I read Mom's and Bud's letters, I knew the outline of their story.

Bud wrote to Mom after he and his wife separated. His first letter—dated October 12, 1988—was accompanied by a photo of Bud and Mom sitting with two other men who were wearing U.S. Navy uniforms. The letter said that one of the men had recently found the photo and "passed it on" to Bud. "It all reminds me that I've been meaning to get in touch for a long time. I expect to be in New York Oct 21-23 and will call then. I'd love to see you again. Best, Bud."

I'd grown up knowing that my mother had a boyfriend in high school named Buddy and that she'd started dating my father when Buddy was in the Army. I didn't know the depth of feeling that she still had for him.

I also didn't know—but would soon learn—that my father had an affair about ten years after he and Mom got married.

Mom had assumed that she and Dad would be monogamous for life. She didn't envision affairs being part of their marriage and was enormously hurt when she learned about it. Then Dad got sick. Mom went outside the marriage once while he was ill. After he recovered, each of them had at least one more assignation.

Bud's reemergence marked the only time that either of my parents discussed their sex life with me, which was once more than I felt comfortable with. When I asked Dad why he'd had that first affair, he answered, "I don't know."

In the preface to his posthumously published autobiography, Mark Twain wrote, "In this autobiography, I shall keep in mind the fact that I am literally speaking from the grave because I shall be dead when the book issues from the press. I can speak thence freely. When a man is writing a book dealing with the privacies of his life—a book which is to be read while he is still alive—he shrinks from speaking his whole frank mind. It has seemed to me that I could be as frank and free and unembarrassed as a love letter if I knew that what I was writing would be exposed to no eye until I was dead, and unaware, and indifferent."

Mom, Dad, and Bud are now gone. The next few pages are reconstructed in part from Mom's and Bud's love letters.

Mom met with Bud on his first full day in New York. They were sixty-two years old. Their hair was gray. Their faces were lined. They weren't kids anymore. But being together, they felt young again.

There's a song in *Follies*—"In Buddy's Eyes"—by Stephen Sondheim with the lyric:

> *In Buddy's eyes, I'm young, I'm beautiful.*
> *In Buddy's eyes, I don't get older.*

Mom and Bud had found the fountain of youth in each other. Later, he would write to her about seeing her for the first time when they were in fourth grade "in the gym, bouncing, catching, and throwing a ball." And a day when they were in eleventh grade: "You in a green plaid skirt, sweater, bobby sox, flashed me a brilliant smile. I was dazzled and never recovered."

Mom took the train into the city and met with Bud again on his second day in New York. And the third. Their letters make it clear that they consummated their relationship (which they hadn't done when they were young) at the Hotel Beverly where he was staying. Then Bud went back to London with the promise to return before the end of the year.

In the weeks that followed, Bud frequently called my mother during the day when my father was at the office. But their primary communication was by letter.

Bud's letters tended to include descriptions of what he was writing and the external activities of each day in addition to thoughts about love. Comparing himself to Odysseus, he described his lifelong passion for my mother as "positively Homeric" and added, "We shall not be separated again. We've wandered forty years in an existential wilderness, both of us, separately. It would be insane, folly, if we let anything get between us now."

"You were so pretty," he wrote. "You are beautiful now. You were sweet then. Now you are tender. We loved then, but it was young, incomplete. I don't feel eighteen now, although I forget things, walk on air, think only of you. If we can't bear to be parted from each other, then we won't. I have always loved you."

My mother's letters were equally passionate.

"I feel so happy. There's a glow and an excitement and warmth and tenderness and so much more. This must be love. I've even started reading poetry, which I haven't done in years. Whatever happens, this is the most important experience of my life . . . You will have to be mature enough for both of us from now on. I feel that I've lost my balance and judgment because I don't think I could bear to be parted from you again. . . . Today I was crying for all the years of love we missed. But we'll make up for it."

The Oscar Hammerstein lyric that accompanied Jerome Kern's melody in *All the Things You Are* was alive in Mom and Bud. They were the promised kiss of springtime, the breathless hush of evening, the angel glow that lights a star. If they had met for the first time when they were in their sixties, it's unlikely that they would have had anything close to the same feelings between them. But fairy tales aren't bound by the same rules as reality.

Letters sent between New York and London in 1988 took anywhere from three days to three weeks to arrive and didn't necessarily arrive in the order in which they were sent. Bud lived at 6 Montagu Place in London. Mom's letters to him were occasionally misdirected to 6 Montagu Square. After receiving three letters from Bud in one day, Mom wrote back, "The letter that touched me most was about your having lived so much of your life with so little love. I promise you that I'll love you very much for the rest of my life."

There's probably no good way to cheat on one's spouse and fall madly in love with someone else. My mother handled the situation particularly poorly. She was consumed by passion and desperate to escape the quicksand that she felt she'd been suffocating in for years. With Bud's reappearance, her old way of life was now intolerable. And she behaved (as she later put it) "like a spoiled sixteen-year-old."

Rather than discuss the situation with Dad or pursue her liaison with Bud discreetly, she confided in an ever-widening circle of family and friends in what became a conspiracy of sorts against my father.

By early November, Mom was talking openly about Bud with her brother and one of her closest friends (Anne Fergenson, who was twenty-seven years younger than Mom). When the family gathered for Thanksgiving, I felt a strange vibe but didn't know what it was. My mother seemed to be only half there. But she hadn't taken me into her confidence yet.

"I think my emotions are dangerously close to the surface," she wrote to Bud. "I find it awfully hard to behave with Si the way I have for the past 43 years."

Bud returned to New York in mid-December and was in the city for four days. Mom told Dad that she'd be in the city each day for a bridge tournament.

"After the four happiest days of my life," Mom wrote to Bud after he'd gone back to London, "the world looks very gray. We may be getting 12 inches of snow. Thank God we didn't get it when you were here. I don't know how long I can hold out here. Last night, Si asked me if anything was the matter and I mumbled something about an old-age crisis."

If Thanksgiving was strange, Christmas was stranger. It was clear that something was wrong. Mom was saying things like "there might be some changes ahead." I didn't know what those change were. But it was starting to sound like she was planning to leave Dad. I asked her directly what was going on and she told me about Bud. With a caveat. She hadn't made up her mind yet. But if I told Dad, she'd be "out the door."

In the days that followed, Mom told my brother and sister about Bud. Soon she was telling almost everyone except Dad.

"I suppose what I'm really depressed about is telling Si," she wrote to Bud. "But somehow, this all has to work out. We love each other too much to let it go."

Bud wrote back, "My life from here on depends on your love."

My parents' closest friends were a couple named Vera and Albert Reegen. Vera had known my father since college. My mother had confided in her with the same warning she'd given to the rest of us.

"If you tell Si, I'm out the door."

"I talked with Vera today," I told Mom. "You're making co-conspirators out of all of us and it's demeaning to Dad. Either you tell him, or Vera and I will."

So, Mom told Dad that she was having an affair with Bud, and that she hadn't made up her mind as to what she was going to do in the long run but she was very unhappy in the marriage.

I think, by then, Dad knew but didn't want to know.

The next day, I had lunch with my father at a restaurant near his office. I was closer to Mom than I was to Dad. But when Bud reentered her life, I felt protective of my father. My biggest fear—and I wasn't alone in worrying about it—was that, if Mom left, it would trigger another debilitating depression.I began the lunch by telling Dad what I knew about Mom and Bud and when I'd learned it. Dad was focused on Bud's reappearance in Mom's life, not the loneliness she felt in their marriage. He said he hoped that Mom would stay. We talked about things Dad might do toward that end, although I had the feeling that whatever happened next would be beyond his control.

Then Dad said something that astounded me. It was a question, actually.

Earlier in this book, I wrote that leaving the law to write was probably the best decision I've made in my life. A decision that came close in terms of importance was my going into therapy. When I turned forty, I was starting to feel as though life might be passing me by. My career was going well. I had good friends and an active social life. But I'd always told myself that I wanted to get married and have children. And there I was, still single, in yet another relationship with a woman (a remarkable woman) who some part of me knew I wasn't going to marry.

So maybe the problem was me.

A woman I'd dated years before who became a lifelong friend was married to a psychiatrist. He gave me the name of another psychiatrist who he respected. And a new journey began. Therapy made me a better person and a happier one.

I'd told Mom and Dad when I went into therapy. Now I was sitting at lunch with my father, discussing his crumbling forty-three-year marriage and all of the implications that had for our family.

This was a man who was not unfamiliar with the mental health system.

"Have you mentioned this situation to your therapist?" Dad asked.

When I had lunch with my father, I told him that, while I hoped he and Mom would stay together, they might consider a trial separation. That night, I said the same thing to Mom.

Meanwhile, Bud and his wife had been living separately for nine months. Each of them had retained an attorney, and his wife had asked that their separation become a divorce as soon as possible.

Bud's wife now knew about Bud seeing my mother. One of their sons had told her.

"Jackie called the other night," Bud wrote to my mother. "Ostensibly about some shipping questions, really to reproach me for not having told her about 'Ellie, your dream girl.' She suggested that our marriage had been false because I had always been in love with you. It was a pretty good marriage for many years. But it is true that I have always loved you."

Soon after that, my mother made an appointment with an attorney to discuss her own situation. After meeting with the lawyer, she wrote to Bud, "He said that he usually tells women or men who come to him for a divorce to try a marriage counselor. In our case, he could only say 'Go for it.'"

Bud wanted to go for it. Immediately. His marriage to Jackie was effectively over. He was ready to leave his flat in London and move to New York to live with Mom.

Mom's situation was more complicated. Despite her passion for Bud and the loneliness of her marriage, she wasn't ready yet to leave Dad.

One of the most painful experiences in life is ending a relationship with someone you care about. Mom had stayed with Dad throughout his illness. He was a kind, gentle man. Despite their extra-marital affairs, she believed in the institution of marriage. They'd shared more than forty years together. And she was scared at the thought of leaving the security of a world she knew for a less certain life.

Her letters told the tale.

"I was up for hours last night thinking about the impossibility of leaving Si. I can't help it. And I have to tell you what I'm thinking because I can't really talk to anyone else about it . . . I've never been happier or more miserable in my life. Sometimes I feel in the middle of a bad dream instead of the most wonderful love affair anyone could have."

Bud did his best to reassure her.

"Of course you're fearful of change. There is so much we don't know: how we'd tolerate setbacks, depression, illness, how we respond in crisis. There are huge chunks of biography we are still learning. But at bottom, we are what we were at 16-18. You are still loving, funny, bold in some things, cautious and rule-bound in others, risk-taking but risk-averse. Above all, we love each other. This does not mean that going off together doesn't entail risks. But I've lived so much of my life with so little love that it's easy for me to say that's a risk well worth taking."

"I'm so very grateful that you wrote to me last October," my mother responded. "It took you 45 years. All I can say is, you were worth waiting for . . . I feel like we're really going to happen. I just can't imagine life without you anymore. I realize that we'll have to go through a lot in the beginning with other people and details, but that's all unimportant . . . Part of me is pushing forward while part of me is pulling back, which I guess is called a conflict. I'm aware that some parts of my letters make me sound like an indecisive flake. But deep down, the real me expects to be with you . . . I'm really not afraid of dying as much as I used to be because I've done at least part of what I was put in this world to do, which is to love you."

Before my grandmother died, she'd had a maid named Bridie, who was with her for twenty years. Bridie, who I'm certain never kissed a man in her life, was akin to a living saint. A facetious comment that my father made about her spoke volumes to my mother.

"Had a funny exchange with Si about whether to buy a new dishwasher because ours is getting old and feeble," my mother wrote to Bud. "Would he want a new one if I wasn't here? He said that he was planning to marry Bridie if I left and she would want one, so to get it. Isn't it interesting that he plans to replace me with my mother's maid."

Bud came back to New York in late January (three months after reconnecting with Mom). He was in the city for four days before flying to Washington D.C. and then San Francisco to visit two of his sons.

"What a dreamlike blissful time with you," Mom wrote in a letter she sent to him in care of one of his sons. "I never can decide which was the best day we spent together because they are all perfect . . . Spoke to Tom, who suggested that maybe it was tough on his father to have me around, that perhaps I should move out now. But Si is of the opinion that time may make me 'come to my senses' and get over this 'obsession' for you."

By then, Bud had decided to not renew his lease in London and move to New York. If Mom moved in with him, that would be nirvana. If not, he'd rent a furnished apartment on his own and continue to pursue her. He was in the city again for a week in mid-February and arranged for a six-month sublet on a one-bedroom apartment.

Mom still hadn't committed to leaving Dad.

"No promises I can't deliver on," she said.

That led to frustration on Bud's part. "It's like a damn football game with the score changing hands on every exchange of the ball," he wrote.

Then another factor came into play. Mom was drinking too much.

Alcohol had long been a curse in our family.

There was a time when my mother's parents were social drinkers. During the Prohibition Era, they hired someone to come to their apartment and make whiskey in the bathtub. "If we're served liquor when we go to someone else's home," my grandmother told my grandfather, "we have to serve liquor when they come to ours."

My grandfather started drinking heavily when he was in his late sixties. After ten years of excess, he stopped. He believed that drinking in moderation was good but came to the understanding that he couldn't drink in moderation. He started taking Antabuse—an alcohol-abuse deterrent that works by blocking the breakdown of alcohol and causing unpleasant side effects (think vomiting) when even a small amount of alcohol is consumed. Now, instead of thinking that he shouldn't drink, he couldn't drink.

Around the time that my grandfather started taking Antabuse, my grandmother upped her alcohol intake. He'd been a morose drunk. She was a nasty one. In later years, her drinking spiraled out of control.

I'd gone to my grandmother's apartment for dinner every three weeks or so after my grandfather died. Finally, I told her, "I don't want to see you like this. I love you and have so many wonderful memories of you. For as long as I can remember, you've been a cornerstone in my life. But if you're drunk every time I come for dinner, I'm not coming anymore."

"Then don't come," she said.

So, I stopped going to my grandmother's for dinner. Several months passed. Then the telephone rang.

"I'd like to invite you for dinner," my grandmother said. "If you come, I won't drink that night."

I never saw her drunk again. Some people never saw her sober.

A few years later, my grandmother was at a friend's home for dinner. She was drunk. When a person is drunk, they tend to chew their food less carefully than they should before swallowing. And some of the throat muscles relax.

My grandmother choked on a piece of chicken. She was in a coma for two days and died without ever regaining consciousness.

My mother was devastated. "There were things we still had to say to each other," she told me.

My uncle inherited my grandparents' alcoholic genes. He was a heavy drinker and tended to get hostile in a passive-aggressive way whenever he had too much to drink (which, in his later years, was almost every night). Then he'd zone out, which meant he wasn't much fun to be with.

I was never a drinker beyond an occasional beer, glass of wine, champagne at celebrations, or a once-a-year margarita.

When it came to drugs, my class year in school was the last of the old generation. I knew that some classmates smoked "pot" (as it was called). But it was largely under wraps. I never saw it. And I had all the excuses for not engaging.

"I'm naturally high . . . I don't need something like that to enjoy music . . . Or food . . . Or sex."

Three months after I started clerking for Judge Croake, I was dating a woman who insisted that we share a joint. If I recall correctly, a sexual incentive was involved. I'd never been a cigarette smoker, so I had what might be called "virgin lungs." I coughed a lot that night. But suddenly, lights were flashing, there was music in my brain, we were making love, and I said to myself, "This is kind of cool."

Let's estimate that I've taken a puff once a week since then.

My parents were social drinkers. Mom had given up cigarette smoking at age fifty-five (which she said was the hardest thing she ever did). As the divide between her and my father widened, she found herself making lists of things to talk about over dinner with Dad so there wouldn't be too many empty silences. And she'd have a drink or two right before he got home.

"Each morning when I woke up," Mom later said, "I promised myself that I'd measure out what I drank that night and not have what would be more than two drinks in a restaurant. But then five o'clock came and my resolve weakened."

She knew what drinking had done to her parents. She went to an Alcoholics Anonymous meeting but decided that she didn't want to stop.

"Drowning one's troubles in vodka feels good at the time," she wrote to Bud. "It isn't a great way to deal with problems, but what a temptation."

As Mom's drama with Bud unfolded, she and I had several telephone conversations where it was clear to me that she'd had too much to drink. Finally, I told her that I thought she was drinking too much. It was an unpleasant conversation and ended on an angry note.

The next day, Mom called.

"You're right," she said.

One day later, she wrote to Bud, "Today was the first day I haven't had a drink in years."

At age sixty-three, Mom gave up drinking. She had incredible willpower. For the rest of her life, her alcoholic intake was limited to an occasional wine spritzer.

"I never blamed my drinking on anything or anyone but myself," she said later. And she told me, "You were the first person to tell me I was drinking too much. Other people either didn't notice or didn't care enough to say anything about it. Thank you."

Bud's sublet in New York was scheduled to begin on March 20, 1989—five months after he had reconnected with Mom. As his arrival neared, she wrote to him almost every day.

"I think of you all the time and will be very happy when you get here . . . I feel that I've let you down already with my indecision. Of all the people in the world, you are the one I would least like to hurt . . . I'm not sure you should even want to join your life with someone who is behaving as erratically as I have . . . Si is giving me a hard time. He brought me flowers for the third night in a row. I said to him that I'd rather he yell at me . . . Please, God (if I believed in Him or Her and wish I did), let us have a happy ending."

"I mustn't press," Bud wrote back. "You must leave to come to me when you feel you're ready, not bound by a calendar. My return to New York binds you to nothing. I want you to come to me more than I've ever wanted anything. But I want you to come joyously and freely and wholeheartedly . . . It's not like it was in 1945. Then I thought I'd never mattered much, was a juvenile episode cast aside for serious matters. Now there's an intensity to my need for you that overwhelms me."

As March 20 approached, my mother picked up the key to Bud's sublet and began readying the apartment for him. She bought a typewriter table (the one "absolutely essential" piece of furniture he said he needed) and started cleaning. Then she stocked the apartment with paper towels, toilet paper, Kleenex, and other mundane essentials.

She told my father when Bud would be arriving and resolved to herself that she wouldn't lie anymore about playing bridge in New York when she was with Bud.

"I think that, after you arrive," she wrote, "Si will get so irritated at the amount of time I spend with you that he may blow up and tell me I have to make up my mind."

If that happened, she'd choose Bud.

Mom's final letter to Bud in London was dated March 11, 1989. "I guess this will be my last letter to 6 Montagu Place," she wrote. "I'm terribly excited about your coming yet anxiety ridden about what will happen."

That anxiety (and indecision) continued after Bud moved to New York. It was a painful time for Mom, Dad, and Bud.

Bud's six-month sublet expired with no decision on my mother's part. He took another sublet.

Finally, Mom took the advice of Anne Fergenson (who had become her closest confidant).

"Stop worrying about Si and Bud and do what's best for you," Anne counseled. "They'll survive."

In early January 1990, fourteen months after Bud reappeared in her life, my mother left my father to live with Bud. She took almost nothing from the house other than her clothes and some other personal belongings. As much as possible, she wanted Dad's physical environment to remain intact.

Mom and Bud rented a two-bedroom apartment on East 75th Street in Manhattan and furnished it from scratch.

"I've found my soulmate," Mom told me just before she left. "I start a sentence and Bud can finish it for me."

Bud's four sons reacted to Mom with varying degrees of acceptance (or lack thereof). My brother, sister, and I had divergent views on our family's upheaval. We'd hoped that Mom and Dad would work things out in a way that enabled them to stay together. But that's where the similarity ended.

Jim was accepting of Bud and invited Mom and Bud to spend a week at his home in Oregon. He wasn't being disloyal to Dad. He was acknowledging the new status quo and letting Mom know that he wanted her to be happy and loved her.

I didn't question Mom's right to leave Dad but had issues with the way she'd done it. I also felt protective toward Dad and wanted to avoid pouring salt in his wounds. That meant continuing to see Mom but, for the time being, not engaging with Bud.

Lise had been harsh in criticizing Mom as her affair with Bud evolved and refused to speak to Mom for two years after Mom left. I told Lise that I thought she was being punitive and cruel, at which point she also stopped speaking to me.

Mom and Bud's new life harkened back to their old one. They reconnected with friends from Fieldston and revisited other touchstones from their youth. Mom even went to a football game with Bud when Dartmouth played Columbia at Baker Field in New York. She had zero interest in football. But for Bud, going to the game was like going back in a time machine with Ellie.

And Mom loved living in New York. The city girl was back in the city.

After Mom and Bud had been together for several months, I took them up on their standing invitation to meet him. We had late-afternoon drinks at their apartment. Bud had read one of my books, which I took as a good-faith effort on his part to build a bridge between us. We talked about writing and politics, and I thought he tended toward the pedantic. Or phrased differently, given the opportunity, Bud might have lectured Frank Sinatra about singing. But that could have been because he was nervous about meeting me and wanted to impress.

In retrospect, I should have spent more time with Bud than I did. I only saw him once more after that. Anne Fergenson got married and invited Mom, Dad, Bud, and me to the wedding. I chatted with Mom and Bud during the cocktail hour and sat with my father during the meal.

Dad was eight years older than Mom and Bud. I think he'd had an image in his mind of Bud looking a bit like Gregory Peck. Instead, he saw an average-looking, middle-aged man with gray hair and a slightly bent gait.

"He looks much older than I thought he'd look," Dad said.

Meanwhile, Mom and Bud were adjusting to their new life. They'd spent relatively little time together before getting their apartment. And that time had been in a supercharged environment, not a routine everyday existence.

Now everything seemed to be going well until . . .

"You don't sound good," I said to Mom one day on the phone.

"I'm fine."

"What's the matter?"

"I don't know."

"Yes, you do."

"Where should I start?"

Bud could be overbearing, Mom said. He was a better talker than listener. There were times when his intensity was a bit much.

"I start a sentence and Bud interrupts me."

But Mom cared about Bud. She really did. I think that, given the opportunity, they would have stayed together. They had a lot in common and Bud's feelings for her were a powerful aphrodisiac. Mom meant it when she said, "The look on Bud's face when I come home and walk into the apartment means the world to me."

Then the decision on their future was made for them. Bud was diagnosed with lung cancer.

A horrible ordeal followed. I won't go into the details of dying. There will be more of that later in this book. It's enough to say here that Mom was Bud's primary caregiver and stayed with him until he died on June 24, 1992 (her forty-seventh wedding anniversary). He was sixty-six years old.

Thirty years later, I was going through Mom's belongings after she died and found a stack of condolence letters that she received after Bud's death. One of them was from a friend of Bud's who wrote to Mom, "Even when Bud was dying, he was happier than I'd ever seen him because he was with you."

Chapter IV

There are places in this narrative where I've been hard on my father. He had limited emotional insight. He didn't dwell on feelings or have heart-to-heart talks. But he did the best he could at everything he did. People liked him. He had a warm smile that reflected his better self.

When Mom left Dad to live with Bud, friends and family rallied around my father. There were telephone calls to see how he was doing and invitations for dinner. He started dating.

If Dad had asked Mom to move back to Larchmont after Bud died, she might have gone. And if she'd asked to come back, he probably would have taken her. But underneath it all, they felt that they were happier living apart. They became friends, having dinner and coming to family celebrations together.

During Mom and Dad's marriage, they'd shared a joint bank account but held their stocks separately. That way, both of them had been free to invest the way they wanted. The deed to the house was in both of their names. When Mom left to live with Bud, she told Dad that he could live in the house without paying her a dime as long as he maintained it.

Under New York law, when a married person dies, the surviving spouse is entitled to at least one-third of the estate regardless of what the deceased person's will says. Neither Mom nor Dad had filed for divorce. After Mom left, Dad drafted a new will that cut her down to this one-third share and he put her share in trust, meaning that she'd get the income on it for life but couldn't touch the underlying funds. Jim, Lise, and I were to split the other two-thirds of Dad's estate outright and inherit the rest when Mom died. I was to be the executor under Dad's will and also the trustee for Mom's trust. He'd given me a copy of his will after he signed it.

Several months after Bud died, Dad and I had lunch.

"I've been thinking about changing my will again," he said. "Your mother and I are getting along well [in conversations between us, he always referred to Mom as "your mother"]. She stood by me when I was sick, and I'd like her to have a financial cushion when she's old. How would you feel if I left my whole estate in trust for her so she has the income for life?"

"I think that's a lovely idea," I said. And I meant it.

At age seventy-five, Dad was enjoying life. He liked working as a lawyer, was socially active, and kept the backyard looking like a conservatory garden.

On the morning of April 23, 1993, Mom telephoned me. She hadn't been able to reach Dad on the phone the night before. She'd just tried him at the office, and he wasn't there. Worse, when Mom called the office, Dad's secretary told her that he hadn't been at work the day before.

Dad had a history of TIAs (transient ischemic attacks). A TIA results from the temporary blockage of blood flow to the brain and is caused by a clot that quickly dissolves or dislodges on its own. The most common symptoms of a TIA are weakness or numbness in the face, an arm, or leg; slurred or garbled speech; loss of balance or coordination; and confusion. The symptoms last briefly and don't cause significant permanent damage. More seriously, roughly one in three people who experience a TIA eventually suffer a stroke.

Several years earlier when Mom and Dad were living together, he came home from playing tennis and Mom asked how the game had been. Dad couldn't remember. If he'd been working in the garden that afternoon and she asked the same question, he would have answered "fine," and no one would have known there was a problem. Mom took him to the hospital, where he was diagnosed as having had a TIA and put on a blood thinner.

The summer after Mom left, Dad was working in the garden. This time, the issue wasn't memory. He kept dropping a pair of pruning shears. Again, he was diagnosed as having had a TIA. His doctor prescribed Coumadin (a stronger blood thinner than the one he'd been on). But he had a bad reaction to the Coumadin and was taken off it.

Mom and I both urged Dad to see an experienced neurologist. But he liked the doctor he was seeing and was stubborn.

Now . . . Mom and I thought Dad might be dead.

I called the police and they went over to the house. The front door was locked. They forced their way in. Dad was lying on a towel on the bedroom floor. From the look of things, he'd been doing his morning exercises when he suffered a massive stroke. He'd been lying on the floor for twenty-six hours.

Dad was hospitalized. He couldn't walk or use his left arm and was cognitively impaired. The best rehabilitation facility in the New York metropolitan area at the time was Rusk Institute at NYU. Dad's internist told us that there was no way Dad could get into Rusk. He was too old and too damaged. Rusk's resources could be put to better use on a younger patient.

I believe in triage and the efficient use of medical resources. But this was my father. A friend who worked at Rusk did me a favor. A big one. When I thanked her afterward, she told me, "I didn't do much, really. All I did was go into the office and tell them to put your father's name at the top of the acceptance list."

At Rusk, Dad learned to walk again but still couldn't use his left arm. He could count to ten but couldn't add two plus three. He couldn't read. In some respects, his thought processes were similar to those of a five-year-old. He also suffered from aphasia—the inability to express himself through speech the way that he once had.

The brain is a strange filing cabinet. After his stroke, Dad couldn't enunciate names.

"What's my name?" I'd ask.

He'd shrug.

"Is my name Richard?"

"No."

"Is my name George?"

"No."

"Is my name Tom?"

"Yes."

"What's my name?"

He couldn't say it.

What he could and did say was, "This is the worst thing ever to me."

My father was no longer capable of living on his own. Mom and I resolved to do whatever we could to ensure that he had as much dignity and comfort and suffered as little as possible in whatever time he had left. Several health care professionals had told us that a nursing home called Mary Manning Walsh (located several blocks from Mom's apartment) offered the best hope for Dad to have an acceptable quality of life. We arranged for him to be admitted there.

Nursing homes are grim places. If you're thinking nice, cheerful, relaxing, pleasant—forget it. They're home to a sad endgame no matter how competent and compassionate the staff might be.

Mom and I went with Dad on the day he was transferred from Rusk to Mary Manning Walsh. His new roommate was a man about his age who, like Dad, had difficulty speaking. A staff member gave us a tour of the facilities. All of the other residents, like Dad, were impaired in one way or another. That's why they were in a nursing home.

Mom's eyes teared up.

After the tour, we went back to Dad's room.

"It's awful," he said.

There was no indecision on Mom's part.

"Si, I promise you, we'll get you out of here."

I stayed with Dad in his room. Mom left Mary Manning Walsh, went to the management office in the building where she lived, and told the managing agent that she wanted to rent an apartment for her husband. She described Dad's condition and explained that they were separated. She said she'd arrange for him to have twenty-four-hour-a-day care at home and would co-sign any necessary financial guarantees. Dad didn't fit the profile for the type of tenant that building management wanted. But there are laws against discrimination on the basis of disability in New York.

Then Mom began asking friends for recommendations regarding live-in care.

"Whatever it costs, we'll do it," she said.

From that point on, Mom oversaw Dad's health care and living arrangements. I shut down his law practice. We handled his finances together and put the house in Larchmont on the market. Mom made lists of who should get what from the house. First, she chose furniture, household appliances, and quite a few of Dad's personal belongings for his apartment. Then she gave things to Jim, Lise, and me and kept other belongings of sentimental value for herself.

We made trip after trip to the house. Before it was sold, Mom and I had to go through forty-one years of accumulated belongings. Some of it was junk that I piled high on the curb for the sanitation department to haul away after each visit.

A moving company was scheduled to come to the house at eight thirty one morning to pick up furniture for shipping to Dad's apartment and other destinations. The telephone and cable service to the house had been cut off. Very few people had cell phones in those days, and Mom wasn't one of them. She spent the night before the movers came alone in the house and said later that it was one of the most unsettling experiences of her life. A lot of memories rattled around with her that night.

There were belongings that nobody in the family wanted— a lot of furniture, air conditioners, household appliances, and the like. We gave those to the New York City Partnership for the Homeless. Three men came to the house in a truck to haul away the donation. While we were loading things into the truck, a neighbor called the police to report a possible robbery. A cop came but was satisfied that nothing was amiss.

Dad's new home was a two-bedroom apartment several floors below Mom's. He could be left alone for up to an hour but had a live-in 24-hour-a-day caregiver who was with him five days a week. A second caregiver covered the other two days.

Mom had spent two years caring for Bud when he was dying of cancer. That ordeal had ended one year earlier. A lot of separated spouses in her position would have looked at Dad, said, "Oh, that's so sad," and not made the commitment she made. She went to Dad's apartment for lunch or dinner every day, took him to doctor appointments, and brought him to occasional social engagements. She had a choice to make. And she made a good one.

Dad being incapacitated by a stroke evoked memories of his earlier, debilitating depression. I'd been too young back then to share the burden of his breakdown with my mother in a constructive way. This time I was able to help.

Parents with a cognitively challenged child have to lower the expectations they once had and concentrate on making their child as happy and productive as possible. The same was true of dealing with Dad in his new condition.

When my father was a boy, going to a restaurant was reserved for special occasions. After he was in his new apartment, I took him out for lunch fairly often. We'd walk for a block or two in his neighborhood. He'd stop and look in all the restaurant windows. Eventually, something would strike his fancy—often, an ordinary diner—and we'd go inside.

One day, Dad's walking was steadier than usual. He struggled with words a few times, but the conversation was flowing pretty well.

He's getting better, I told myself.

Then we came to a restaurant with window frames that were painted green. Dad stopped and looked inside.

"It a nice restaurant," he said. "But there's no door to get in."

And I realized he was broken in ways that I'd never understand.

One evening, Mom asked him, "Are you glad you're alive?"

"Sure," Dad answered.

Eight months after my father suffered his stroke, his regular caregiver had a family emergency and had to take an unscheduled night off. Her backup was unavailable, so Mom slept over at Dad's that night. Shortly after he woke up in the morning, he lost the ability to talk. Mom called 911 and he was taken to Lenox Hill Hospital. At the hospital, he suffered another stroke, this one more damaging than the ones that had come before.

Dad was alive. He could breathe on his own. But that was all. There was virtually no brain activity. When I got to the hospital, he was connected to feeding tubes with no hope of becoming cognizant again.

Years before, Dad had designated me as his health care proxy. His instructions were clear:

> "I direct that any medical or surgical treatment that serves only to prolong the process of my dying be withheld and/or withdrawn if I should be in any mental or physical condition with no reasonable expectation of recovery without the loss of the ability to have a productive and meaningful life. These instructions apply if, by way of example only, I should be in a coma or in a state of permanent unconsciousness with only remote hope of survival without serious permanent brain damage, or if I should have a terminal condition or suffer a severe stroke or have any other condition or disease which prevents me from having a productive and meaningful life. In any such situation, I direct that all life sustaining treatment be withheld or withdrawn."

The hospital wouldn't disconnect Dad from the feeding tubes and let him die in the hospital. He could live in his vegetative state for weeks, maybe months. But they were willing to remove the tubes and send him home to die.

We brought Dad home. He was filled with morphine to negate the possibility of any physical pain. Death came six days later, on January 14, 1994. He was seventy-six years old.

The next day, I went to Riverside Memorial Chapel to

identify Dad's body. Ravaged by strokes, shriveled by six days of dehydration, he looked like he was ninety-five years old when he died. Thirty years later, I can't get that image out of my mind.

My father had said he didn't want a funeral and that he should be cremated with his remains scattered in the rose garden in our backyard. Mom had signed a contract to sell the house by then. But the closing hadn't occurred yet, so there were no complications in following his wishes.

My brother and his children (Cathy, age ten, and Jessica, six) flew in from Oregon to join Mom and me in Larchmont.

"I feel sad for people that they have to die," Jessica told us.

After Dad's stroke, I'd found a poem in a leather box on top of his bureau. While we were gathered in the rose garden, I read part of it:

> *I do not want a gaping crowd*
> *To come with lamentations loud,*
> *When I am dead.*
>
> *Nor do I want my words and ways*
> *Rehearsed by them with tardy praise,*
> *When life has fled.*
>
> *I only want the faithful few*
> *Who stood through good, and evil too;*
> *True friendships' test.*
>
> *Just those who sought to find the good,*
> *And then, as only true friends could,*
> *Understood the rest.*

People talk about "ashes," but that's a misnomer. The

flames in a crematory raise the temperature to as much as two thousand degrees and reduce human remains to bone fragments. When the burning is complete, the bone fragments are pulverized.

Dad's remains had been packed by the crematorium in a white plastic bag inside a black plastic box. I'd transferred them to a green cardboard box imprinted with gold celestial symbols on the lid.

We scattered Dad's remains in the rose garden, burned the cardboard box, and sprinkled the residue of the box around the yard.

Decades later, I revisited the house. A friend told me it was for sale and that the broker had scheduled an "open house." I went out of curiosity and with the thought of rekindling old memories. The house was empty. The owner had moved out. I told the broker that I'd lived there as a boy, and he said I could look around.

The house had been extensively remodeled. Walls had been knocked down and rooms reconfigured. The rose garden where my father spent so many hours planting and pruning was gone. There was only grass.

"Dad is down there," I thought. And my mind wandered back to an evening I'd spent with him about a month before he died.

I was at Dad's apartment for dinner. He was struggling with words that night, and I played a game with him that I often played on the telephone with Jessica.

"I just put orange juice on your head," I'd tell Jessica.

"Now I put juice on your head, Uncle Tom."

"Oh, no! Yuck! There's juice all over my head. Okay! I just got a towel and wiped it off. My hair is dry. Now I put ice cream on your head."

Jessica and I would go back and forth on the phone with

soup, spaghetti, and whatever else she wanted to put on my head until she decided it was time to move on to a conversation with Nerdo, the nice monster, the nasty monster, or one of the other characters I'd created to entertain her.

Dad's stroke had left him with what, in some respects, was the mind of a young child. I explained the game to him.

"I put juice on your head," he said.

"Oh, no! What a mess."

I wiped my hair with my napkin.

"Okay. Now my head is dry."

"I put spinach on your head," my father blurted out.

We went on and on. Dad roared with laughter. Just before I left, I kissed him on the cheek.

"I love you much," he said.

I've thought about that night many times since then. It was the only time after my father's stroke that I heard him laugh.

And it was the only time ever that he told me he loved me.

But I always knew he loved me.

Chapter V

M om had been living alone for nineteen months when my father died. And she was living the way she wanted to. She loved being back in New York, going to plays, lectures, museums, and concerts. The array of people she came in contact with every day energized her.

She stayed in the same apartment she'd lived in with Bud. The windows faced east and south from the twenty-fourth floor. There were two bedrooms (she and Bud had converted one of them into a den), a living room with a dining area, a small kitchen, and a balcony with lots of sunlight where Mom planted flowers during the growing season.

Before my father suffered his stroke, he'd gone out on occasion with a woman named Doris Rosenberg. After he was incapacitated, Doris invited him to a small dinner party. But there was no way that Dad could go on his own. It would have been like sending a five-year-old onto the streets of New York unprotected. So, Doris invited my mother to come with him.

After my father died, Mom took Doris to a concert at

Lincoln Center as a thank you. Not long after that, Doris telephoned.

"I'm having several people over for dinner," she told my mother. "One of them is a man named Alan Raphael whose wife died right before Si. I think you'd like him."

Mom was sixty-eight years old. The love of her youth who she'd reunited with in middle age was gone. She'd just buried the man who had been her husband for almost a half-century. There was no doubt in her mind that the romantic part of her life was over. But she liked Doris. So, she accepted the invitation.

And her life turned golden.

Alan Raphael was eight years older than Mom. He'd been born and raised in New York, went to college at Cornell, and served in the U.S. Navy during World War II. His career (he was now retired) blended his skills as a mechanical engineer and businessman.

In a twist of fate, it turned out that Alan's parents had played bridge occasionally with my mother's parents. That came to light when he mentioned to my mother that his parents had been named Angus and Gladys.

There aren't many Angus and Gladys Raphaels.

"I know those names," Mom said.

Each year, Alan bought a black, pocket-sized appointment book with his initials and the year embossed in gold on the front. And each year, he put them on a closet shelf after they'd expired. When he died, my mother kept his appointment book for 1994. The entry for Friday, April 29, 1994, reads, "7:00 PM—Doris Rosenberg, Herb M, Naomi M, Elly [sic] H."

Mom and Alan's next get together was on Sunday, May 15. They had lunch at a restaurant called Voulez Vous followed by a bridge date with a couple named Werner and Alice Wolff. I assume they got along well that day because they had dinner together that night. "Elly" appears in Alan's appointment book with increasing frequency after that, soon to become "Ellie."

Alan and his wife were married for forty-six years. It was an unhappy marriage. Before his wife died, Alan had undergone open heart surgery. Recounting that experience, he told my mother, "I remember being wheeled into the operating room before they put me under and not caring whether I lived or died."

"I care," my mother told him.

It wasn't long before Mom was talking with family and friends about a man she'd met. Would I like to have lunch with him? A Sunday, June 26, 1994, entry in Alan's appointment book reads, "12:00—Beach [a local cafe]—Ellie and Tom."

I went not knowing what to expect but telling myself I should do my best to be charming.

First impressions count for a lot. My first impression of Alan was that he was a smart, kind, thoroughly decent man with a wonderful sense of humor; tall with a full head of hair that could be described as silver rather than gray. He could have passed for a star from Hollywood's golden era.

Clearly, my mother and Alan were smitten with each other. I left lunch that day feeling that Mom would be in good hands whenever they were together.

Earlier in this narrative, I mentioned working on a book called *The Black Lights*. I'd always been a sports fan and wanted to write a book about sports. But there was a problem. You can't just walk into Yankee Stadium and talk to the Yankees or Madison Square Garden and talk to the Knicks. Boxing is an open sport. A person can walk into any gym in the country and talk with the fighters who are training there.

The Black Lights was published in 1985. It explored the sport and business of boxing, was well-received by the boxing community, and caught the attention of the mainstream press. With that on my resume, I was approached by Muhammad and Lonnie Ali (Muhammad's wife) through their literary agent. Ali hadn't fought in years. He was showing troubling symptoms from the blows to the head that he'd taken during his long ring journey—most notably, slurred speech. The Alis wanted a book that would put Muhammad's life and accomplishments in perspective. Was I interested?

For twenty months, I devoted myself to researching and writing *Muhammad Ali: His Life and Times.* I had a room in the Ali's home that I stayed in for up to a week at a time. I sat on the sofa in my living room watching tapes of the Rumble in the Jungle and Thrilla in Manila with Muhammad beside me. I traveled with him to places as diverse as the Holocaust Memorial Museum in Washington D.C. and The Grand Mosque in Jakarta.

Being Muhammad's official biographer opened doors. As an adolescent, I'd collected autographs from sports legends like Ted Williams, Hank Aaron, Bill Russell, Wilt Chamberlain, and Jim Brown. Now I was interviewing them and other iconic figures like Betty Shabazz (Malcolm X's widow), Dick Gregory, Alex Haley, Andrew Young, Julian Bond, and James Earl Jones.

Jimmy Carter spoke with me about his decision to send Ali to Africa in the hope of gathering support for the United States boycott of the 1980 Olympic Games in Moscow. Gerald Ford recounted his decision to invite Muhammad to the White House as part of an effort to heal the wounds of racial division, Vietnam, and Watergate that were tormenting America.

"How did you feel meeting Muhammad Ali?" I asked the former president. "How did he strike you?"

"He was a magnificent piece of human flesh," Ford responded.

That was the athlete in Ford talking. Decades earlier, he'd starred on two undefeated University of Michigan football teams that won national championships.

When I sent Ford a transcript of the excerpts from our interview that I planned to use in the book, his "magnificent piece of human flesh" comment was excluded. "I understand exactly what you were saying," I explained. "And Muhammad loved it when I read it to him. But there are people who would take it the wrong way."

I met Bill Clinton twice at the White House with Muhammad, one of those times in the Oval Office. I also had the dubious pleasure of meeting Donald Trump at a dinner in Ali's honor in Atlantic City. At one point during the proceedings, Muhammad leaned over to me and whispered of Trump, "He's not as big as he thinks he is."

Like everyone else in my family and circle of friends, Mom wanted to meet Muhammad. I invited her to my apartment one afternoon when Ali and I were watching fight films together. Muhammad had gotten up from the sofa and was waiting in the foyer when she arrived. Like many people, her reaction was an internalized, "Omigod!"

"You're so much bigger than I thought," Mom said.

Then things got interesting.

"Did you call me a nigger?" Ali demanded.

"No! I said 'bigger.'"

"She called me a nigger," Muhammad announced. And he advanced menacingly toward her, smacking a fist into the palm of his hand.

At that point, Mom could have been forgiven for thinking that her life might have been less complicated if her son had kept his job as a lawyer on Wall Street.

"I said 'bigger,'" she repeated with a modicum of alarm.

Then the smile that the whole world fell in love with spread across Ali's face. He reached out, hugged my mother, and proclaimed, "Got you!"

Neither my mother nor Alan had expected to find romantic love late in their lives. But they found it. Bud had been in large part about Mom's past. Alan was about the present. After a lonely marriage, her husband's breakdown, an emotional roller-coaster ride with Bud, and Dad's stroke, Mom had found safe harbor. She and Alan were totally devoted to each other.

"When I was growing up," Mom later said, "I didn't have a role model in my parents for the best of what love between a man and a woman can be. Si didn't either. I guess a lot of people don't. I was in love with Bud, and I loved him. I really did. But the way I felt about Alan was different from anything I'd felt before. It was serene and exciting, comfortable and romantic. After I met Alan, my life was like a fairy tale."

Alan lived six blocks from my mother. She spent almost every weekend from Friday afternoon through early Sunday evening at his apartment. They traveled together, celebrated birthdays and holidays together, and spent time with each other's family and friends. I looked forward to seeing Alan, both with Mom and just the two of us at the occasional lunches we had together. I didn't have to worry about whether Mom was content on a day-to-day basis. With Alan in her life, I knew she was. She was happier and more serene than I'd ever seen her.

One year, we celebrated Alan's birthday with dinner and dancing at the Rainbow Room—the landmark restaurant that overlooked Manhattan from the sixty-fifth floor of 30 Rockefeller Plaza. The room was a symbol of New York's elegance and grandeur and had been since Mom's youth. In its early years, formal dress was required. Some patrons still wore black tie.

Mom and Alan made a nice couple. They looked like they belonged together. The orchestra was playing. Alan took Mom's hand and started singing in tune with the music:

> *And when I told them how beautiful you are*
> *They didn't believe me. They didn't believe me.*

After they'd known each other for several years, Alan gave my mother a gold wedding band as a symbol of their commitment to each other.

From time to time, they talked about getting married. If one of them had wanted to, the other would have. But they were happy with things the way they were.

One evening, I telephoned Mom. She was crying. Happy crying. She did that sometimes.

"I was just listening to Frank," she explained (Mom was on a first-name basis with Sinatra). "He was singing 'The Second Time Around.'" And Mom started singing: "Love is lovelier the second time around . . . Just as wonderful with both feet on the ground."

Years later, Mom reminisced, "I remember standing next to Alan on an elevator and looking at him and thinking, 'You're everything I ever wanted.'"

Once, when they were walking down the street holding hands, Alan stopped, looked toward the heavens, and said, "Finally!"

After Dad suffered his stroke, Mom and I had put a ritual in place. Each morning, she'd telephone me when she woke up. Sometimes, we'd talk for twenty seconds, sometimes for twenty minutes. The rationale for the calls was that neither of us wanted Mom lying incapacitated in bed or on the floor for hours like Dad had. Her cheery "I'm alive and well" was a welcome start to each day.

One morning, Mom went out without making her ritual telephone call. That night, I told her, "From now on, if you miss a call, I'm fining you a hundred dollars."

There was no need for her to call on weekends when she was with Alan. Both of us figured that he'd notice if she was dead.

Several years passed. Then Mom missed a call. Around ten o'clock, I telephoned her at home (she still didn't have a cell phone). There was no answer. So, I called Alan to see if, even though it was the middle of the week, she'd spent the night with him.

"She didn't," Alan said. "But I spoke with your mother this morning and she said she was going out early. I don't know where she is right now, but I'm sure she's fine."

Which was good news. But I still fined Mom a hundred dollars. A check arrived in the mail several days later, and she never forgot to call me again.

Meanwhile, I had added a new dimension to my writing. The internet was becoming a force in journalism, and I started writing articles about the contemporary boxing scene for several websites. That meant going to fights. A lot of them.

On Saturday, April 17, 2004, I was at Madison Square Garden for a fight card promoted by Don King. It was a long night. I got home late, turned off the ringer on my telephone, and set the alarm for 10:00 a.m.

On Sunday morning when I woke up, the message light on my answering machine was flashing.

I hit "play."

It was my mother. After two words, I knew from her voice that something was wrong.

"It's Mom . . . Alan died."

On Saturday afternoon, Mom and Alan had gone to Philharmonic Hall for a performance by a string quartet. They had an early dinner with friends, went back to Alan's apartment, watched a movie on television, and turned in for the night.

Alan was an early riser. Almost always when my mother woke up, he was sitting at the dining room table, reading the *New York Times*, drinking a cup of coffee. Now he was in bed beside her. His body was cold. He'd had a massive heart attack.

They had ten years together.

My mother lay in bed with Alan, running her fingers through his hair. Then she called 911, left a message on my answering machine, and called one of Alan's children.

I got dressed and went over to Alan's apartment.

"I'm glad I was here," Mom said. "It would have been horrible to think of Alan dying alone and lying there until someone found him. And I'm glad he had a gentle death. Si and Bud had hard ones."

Chapter VI

The seventeenth-century moralist Francois de la Roche-foucauld wrote, "Few people know how to be old."

Mom was seventy-eight when Alan died. She walked a lot, watched her weight, and was partial to chicken and salad. She'd given up smoking and drinking years before. But no one on her side of the family tree had lived past eighty-two (a ripe old age in an earlier era).

She was getting old.

Reading moved to the top of her list of pleasures. She had a particular liking for biographies and memoirs and immersed herself in subjects that interested her. I was charged with going online to order books (new and old) that fueled her habit. She read the *New York Times* each day, *The New Yorker* each week, and had an inexhaustible thirst for knowledge. At age eighty, she enrolled in a class on global politics at NYU.

"One of the secrets to a good old age," she said, "is to keep learning."

She lived alone. Once a week, a housekeeper came to clean the apartment, do the laundry, and handle chores that were too much for Mom to handle. She had always gotten along well with the people who worked in her home. Not one—literally, not one—left unless retirement or other circumstances forced a change.

Soon after Alan died, there was a blip on the radar screen when she began having severe pain in her left hip. That led to hip replacement surgery. One of Mom's better qualities was that she'd never been a complainer. During the rehabilitation period, she complained a lot. And not just about her hip.

Finally, we had a talk.

"Look," I told her. "I know you're unhappy. Alan is gone. It will be a while before you recover from the operation and get back to your normal routine. You're feeling old and devalued. I understand that. But you're important to a lot of people. We love you and we'll get through this together."

Mom took it all in. Then she smiled and said, "This reminds me of when you told me I was drinking too much. Thank you."

Mom's ten years with Alan had given her an inner peace that she hadn't known before. "After Alan," she later reminisced, "I felt that my life was complete. I'd had it all." Remembering him soon became a source of joy rather than sadness.

For much of her life, Mom's sense of self had come in large part from the men she was coupled with—my father, Bud, then Alan. Now she found herself in who she was.

Maya Angelou wrote, "People will forget what you said. People will forget what you did. But people will never forget how you made them feel."

Mom made people feel good about themselves. People who met her wanted to get to know her better.

She grew older gracefully.

Her contentment made her a more emotionally generous person.

She was kind.

She had compassion for other people.

She was appreciative for all the advantages that she'd enjoyed in her life.

She was straightforward. She said what she thought and didn't back down from her point of view. But she was open-minded and willing to look at all sides of an issue. If she decided she was wrong, she'd admit it.

She was formidable.

She could laugh at herself.

She loved being a grandmother. My brother was a single parent with sole custody of his two children for much of their formative years. They lived in Oregon but came to New York for extended visits fairly often.

Mom's relationship with my sister was difficult. "Challenging" (to use Mom's word). She saw less of my sister's son and daughter than she did of my brother's children but kept her heart open to them.

Like all mothers, Mom wanted her children to be happy. But happiness comes in many forms.

When I was young, I assumed that someday I'd be married with children. Neither eventuality has happened so far, and the children part won't. For most of my adult life, I've been a serial monogamist. I lived with a woman once. Some former girlfriends are close friends to this day. I lost contact with others long ago.

There came a time when I realized that I could have a completely fulfilling life without children. My writing ensures that some part of me will be left when the rest of me is gone. As for the "till death do us part" commitment, I'm seventy-seven years old now. That's the same age Alan was when he met my mother.

Mom came to understand that I was living a life that was

right for me.

~

As my mother moved through her eighties, three women played an increasingly important role in her emotional support system.

Anne Fergenson (who by then was Anne Teall), Robin Hoffmann, and Honey Shields were about my sister's age. Each of them thought of Mom as a surrogate mother, and she loved them as though they were her daughters.

Anne and Mom had been friends since the 1970s when they took a course together in economics. Mom frequently gave Anne advice on life which Anne never followed. They talked on the phone almost every night.

Robin and I met in the park on the day that I turned thirty. We went to India and Nepal together that year and have been in each other's lives ever since. Mom and Robin hit it off from the start. Eventually, Robin married, moved to Rhode Island, and had three children. In Mom's later years, she and Robin had long telephone conversations every week. They also sent letters and cards to each other. When Mom died and I emptied out her apartment, I found a drawer full of cards that Robin had sent her. I mentioned it to Robin so she'd know how much the cards meant to Mom, and she told me that she had a similar collection of cards that she'd received from my mother.

"If I could have picked a daughter," one of Mom's cards to Robin read, "she would have been exactly like you."

Honey came into my life several years after I met Robin and has been a regular at family gatherings ever since. Her given name was Hannah (after her paternal grandmother). When she was little, her parents called her Honey as a term of endearment. Very few kids want to be called Hannah, so Honey stuck.

Honey is a giver. She has worked in health care for most of her life, teaching college courses and overseeing recreational therapy for children who've suffered brain tumors and other disabling conditions. In Mom's old age, she saw Honey a lot in family settings.

Our bodies change as we age. Old bodies are very different from young ones. All the things that people say will happen to us when we get old happen when we get old. The only question is to what degree and when.

Mom was one of those fortunate people who enjoyed good health throughout her life. But no one can halt the passage of time.

Eighty turned to eighty-five.

"The years go by so fast," she said.

In her late eighties, Mom started using a cane when she went out.

"People are so nice," she told me. "Strangers stop and help me on the street when I'm trying to get a cab. Neighbors ring my bell and offer to go shopping for me when it snows."

On one occasion, Mom was out doing errands and had a craving for a jelly donut. So, she stopped in a Dunkin Donuts shop a block from her apartment.

"Their donuts aren't very good," she recounted. "But a bad jelly donut is better than no jelly donut."

It was cold so Mom was bundled up in a not-particularly-stylish winter coat. She had a lot of change in her purse. As she waited in line, she started counting nickels and dimes with some pennies thrown in. She also chatted amiably with the woman in front of her before refocusing her attention on her purse.

After Mom ordered her donut (raspberry), she put her money on the counter. The young woman at the cash register waved it off.

"It's been taken care of," she said, pointing to the woman who'd been standing in front of Mom and was now out the door.

"That was such a nice thing to do," Mom told me. "I wish I'd gotten her name and address. I could have sent her something from Tiffany."

We're all in good health until one day we're not.

On Mom's eighty-ninth birthday, she could walk a half mile (ten city blocks) with relative ease. Three months later, walking one block left her exhausted. Her cardiologist—a doctor named Richard Kutnick whom she'd known for years—administered a stress test.

Mom liked Dr. Kutnick. He was competent and caring and always ended appointments with the warning, "Whatever you do, don't fall."

Kutnick reviewed the results of the stress test, thought there was a possible arterial blockage, and arranged for Mom have an angiogram at Lenox Hill Hospital. The procedure was overseen by a cardiologist named Sriram Iyer.

After the angiogram, Dr. Iyer discussed the results with Mom and me.

Mom had an eighty-percent blockage in her right coronary artery. It could be treated with an angioplasty (using a balloon to open the artery, enabling blood to flow more freely) and inserting a stent (which would decrease the chance of the artery narrowing again). The greatest danger in the procedure was that there was considerable calcification in the artery. If a piece of that calcification broke off and flowed unimpeded to Mom's brain, it could result in a catastrophic stroke.

But Mom's other options were worse. Open heart surgery

would incapacitate her for months with no guarantee of success. And if she did nothing, a heart attack was inevitable.

Mom opted for the angioplasty and told Dr. Iyer, "I'm eighty-nine years old. I've had a wonderful life. I love living but I'm not afraid of dying. If I have a stroke in the operating room and it's a bad one, I don't want to wake up."

"I understand," the doctor said.

That wasn't a commitment on his part. But he got the message.

On Thursday, May 28, 2015, I woke up at 5:00 a.m., took a car service to Mom's apartment, and brought her to Lenox Hill Hospital.

"You don't have to bring me," Mom had said several days earlier. "I can get there on my own. It will be enough if you're there afterward."

That was Mom.

"There's not a chance in the world that I won't bring you to the hospital," I told her. "You know that."

We arrived at Lenox Hill at 6:15 a.m. and were taken to a room on the eleventh floor. Mom gave a nurse a list of drugs that I didn't know she was taking for ailments that I didn't know she had.

While we were waiting, Mom told me she loved me and thanked me for being there.

"This is the definition of quality time," I told her. "I'll see you in a few hours."

The operation was a success.

I'd always known that I was likely to outlive my mother. This was the first time that I confronted the inevitability of her dying on an emotional level. I didn't cry the day that Mom died. But I cried the night after her angioplasty.

I knew that someday, probably soon, I'd lose her.

Chapter VII

Shortly before his ninetieth birthday, Larry Merchant (the venerable journalist and TV commentator) observed, "It's easier to get into your eighties than it is to get out of them."

Mom recovered well from her angioplasty. But it doesn't matter who you are. If you live long enough, the struggles of old age will become part of your life. Sixty might be the new fifty. But ninety is ninety. On December 28, 2015, Mom turned ninety.

She had started to look frail and feel more vulnerable.

Five months after her ninetieth birthday, Mom was sitting on the edge of her bed, putting in eyedrops. The next thing she knew, she was on the floor and didn't know how she'd gotten there. There was a trickle of blood from her elbow, and it felt as though she'd hit her head. The cap was still off the eyedrop dispenser. The most likely scenario was that she'd slid off the bed while leaning back to put the eyedrops in and hit her elbow and head on the way down. She telephoned me. She was completely lucid. I took her to see Dr. Kutnick, who examined her and said she could go home.

Ten days later, Mom was having intermittent headaches. An MRI indicated that she'd suffered a small brain bleed. Dr. Kutnick took her off Plavez (a blood-thinner she'd been on) and suggested she see a neurologist named Gerald Smallberg. Smallberg and Kutnick both thought Mom's symptoms were inconsistent with a TIA and assumed that the bleed occurred when she slipped off the bed and hit her head. The bleeding had stopped and, they agreed, was unlikely to cause a future problem.

Six months after that, Mom made her morning telephone call to me and, midway through the conversation, had trouble verbalizing. The problem cleared up while we were talking. I took her to Dr. Smallberg's office. While we were there, the problem reoccurred and Smallberg instructed me to bring her to the emergency room at Lenox Hill Hospital.

Mom was in the hospital for two days of tests.

"The worst one was when they put gunk in my hair [for an encephalogram]," she reported. "I hate having gunk in my hair. And they didn't wash it all out afterward."

The belief after the tests was that Mom had suffered a TIA. Reassuringly, she'd returned to baseline with no sign of lasting damage. The director of stroke services at Lenox Hill told Mom that he was comfortable with her continuing to live alone. I arranged for her housekeeper to spend the next few nights with her at her apartment.

Mom turned ninety-one.

I took to stopping on the street to help elderly people flag down taxis as a consequence of Mom's appreciation for strangers doing the same thing for her.

"The best thing about being in my nineties," Mom told me, "is that I'll never have to go through colonoscopy prep again. At my age, I'm not worrying about five years down the road."

But the medical incidents were coming closer together. A

week after Mom's ninety-first birthday, she told me that she'd been on the phone with a friend and experienced a brief interlude when she'd had trouble verbalizing. Again, I took her to Dr. Smallberg's office. He examined her for forty-five minutes, much of which was devoted to cognitive questioning.

"You made a few mistakes," he told her afterward. "But you're very sharp, incredibly sharp for ninety-one."

Smallberg now thought that at least some of Mom's episodes were the result of atypical migraine headaches. Topomax was added to her list of medications.

Walking was becoming more difficult because of Mom's legs, not her heart. Dr. Alexander Shtilbans (a specialist in movement disorders) diagnosed her as having lower-body vascular Parkinson's caused by a narrowing of blood vessels in the brain.

"There's no muscle stiffness," he told her. "The tremor is mild. It's nothing to write home about."

He prescribed generic Sinemet.

A minor eye procedure had to be rescheduled when the doctor's office called Mom on the day of the appointment and said the doctor was out sick with the flu.

"It could have been worse," Mom told me philosophically. "If I was the one with the flu, the appointment would have been postponed plus I'd have the flu."

It was becoming increasingly difficult for Mom to do things that had once been easy for her to do. Taking the garbage to the incinerator chute on her floor now required significant effort.

But she still loved living. Her mind, as Dr. Smallberg noted, remained incredibly sharp. She adjusted to each new change in circumstances and maintained her independence. For years, she'd been out of her apartment almost every day. At lectures, museums, playing bridge. Now she was most comfortable at home.

"As long as nothing hurts," Mom said, "I'm completely content to sit home and read."

Going to her apartment during the summer was a bit like going into a desert. She liked it hot.

Photos of family and friends were on tables, shelves, bureaus, and anywhere else there was space. Another photo captured the moment when Muhammad Ali reached out to hug Mom in my apartment.

"It impresses the hell out of handymen when they come up to fix something," she said.

After Mom's angioplasty I became more involved with her day-to-day living than before. I won't say day-to-day "care" because she still cared for herself. Mom had put a great deal of time and effort into looking after her own parents in their final years. "When the chips are down," she told me, "either you're there for someone or you're not."

Now I wanted to be there for Mom. I printed out lists of her prescriptions, taped one on the kitchen wall, gave her another for her purse, and updated them with each change. I accompanied her to doctor appointments and, when she thanked me, reminded her, "You took me to a lot of doctors and dentists when I was young."

I went to her apartment for lunch almost every Sunday. Honey usually came with me. She and Mom would talk while I reviewed financial documents that had come in during the week, watered plants, and checked out the apartment to make sure that everything was in order.

One day after I'd spent several hours organizing 1099s and other papers for Mom's annual tax filing and was readying to go home, she said she'd walk out with me because she needed several things from the supermarket.

"I'll go with you," I said.

"You don't have to."

"I know I don't have to. I want to. I can carry things home for you. In fact, you stay here and I'll go alone. It will be easier for you and quicker for me."

"I want to go so I can see what you're getting. I go to the supermarket every day on my own."

At that point, a thought flashed through my mind: "Mom is ninety-one years old. What if I don't see her again?"

So, I went with her to the supermarket, which took a long time because she was moving slowly by then.

"Everyone should have a Tom," one of Mom's friends told her—a statement that she repeated to me at least a hundred times.

She loved reading the books I wrote. As soon as one came back from the printer, I'd give her a copy. She'd read it, we'd talk about it, and it would go on her official "Thomas Hauser bookshelf" (which included foreign-language editions). Mom once noted with pride that she had one of only two known collections of The Complete Works of Thomas Hauser in the world.

My relationship with Muhammad Ali had led to a collaboration with another sports legend. *Arnold Palmer: A Personal Journey* (a large photo book with a lengthy text) shared space with *Muhammad Ali: In Perspective* (my second Ali project) on the coffee table in front of Mom's sofa.

She was also partial to *Finding the Princess*—a novel I wrote in which the protagonist has a rather unsympathetic mother. I wanted to make it clear that *Finding the Princess* wasn't symbolic matricide. Hence the book's dedication, which read, "For Eleanor Hauser, who has become an almost perfect person, and Alan Raphael, her other half."

She loved old movies on television and watched her favorites again and again. "People know how Shakespeare's plays end," she said. "That doesn't keep them from seeing *Romeo and Juliet* and *Macbeth* more than once."

And she loved a good cry. She cried when Eliza Doolittle came back to Henry Higgins at the end of *My Fair Lady*. She cried when Spencer Tracy talked about love at the end of *Guess Who's Coming to Dinner*. She cried when Gaston asked for Gigi's hand in marriage. She cried at the end of *The Best Years of Our Lives*. And keeping current, her eyes teared up when Will proposed to Mac at the end of Season Two of *Newsroom*.

For years, Mom had played bridge at a club called The Regency. Virtually all of her friends from earlier years had predeceased her. But she'd made new ones at the bridge table and advised me, "You should have some friends who are younger than you are. That way, if your old friends die, you'll still have the young ones."

Now Mom no longer wanted the pressure of making plans in advance to play bridge and worrying about getting to the club on time and getting home afterward, particularly if it was raining. She decided to leave The Regency. On her last day there, she and her partner finished first out of a dozen teams in a duplicate bridge tournament. That pleased her. It meant her mind was still sharp.

She'd always loved theater. That too was becoming a burden. She very much wanted to see *Dear Evan Hansen,* which was sold out months in advance. I got two orchestra tickets for a Wednesday matinee through a friend. The first show Mom had seen on Broadway was *Babes in Arms* (the 1937 Rodgers and Hart musical with songs like *Where or When* and *The Lady is a Tramp*).

"If *Dear Evan Hansen* is the last show I go to," Mom said when it was over, "it's a wonderful note to end on."

My grandmother took me to my first Broadway show. I'd just taken my mother to what would be her last.

The older Mom got, the more connected she felt to the world at large and empathized with other people's struggles. It would have been easy for her to sit back and say, "I have a comfortable life, these aren't my problems." But that wasn't her values set. She had a strong sense of social justice and understood that no one is affected by hardship as much as those who have little or nothing to begin with. She knew that hunger isn't about dinner being served an hour late and that real money problems don't center on whether someone can afford to continue their country club membership.

One day, we were out doing errands and passed a homeless woman who was sitting on the sidewalk with several large garbage bags stuffed with her belongings.

"I wonder what she has in the bags," Mom said.

That homeless woman was a person to her.

During one of our telephone calls, Mom told me, "I was aggravated this morning because the water in the building is being turned off for the day so they can clean the water tanks. And then I thought about people in the Bahamas [which had just been savaged by Hurricane Dorian]. Most of them had so little to begin with and now they have nothing but the clothes on their back."

It saddened her that there are people who find satisfaction in hating.

It infuriated her when people said they didn't care about global warming and that life, as far as they were concerned, was about their own pleasure without regard to what might happen after they're gone.

Mom felt that she had a place—an infinitesimally small niche, but a place nonetheless—in the arc of history. She felt privileged to be part of what we call civilization. It troubled her that people are so careless with the future.

She'd always been interested in politics. The bedrock values of Franklin Roosevelt's New Deal were in her blood. She knew that inequities had been visited upon Black Americans and other marginalized people. But she believed in America and its capacity for positive change.

She adored Barack Obama. His decency and eloquence lifted her spirits. Midway through election night in 2008, my telephone rang. It was Mom. And of course, she was crying. "I'm so happy," she said. "We just won Pennsylvania."

Then Donald Trump was elected president. As the abuses of the Trump presidency mounted, it impacted severely on Mom's mood.

"Look at what America is becoming," she said.

What troubled her most was that Trump's election (and that of the Republican-controlled Congress that joined him in power) wasn't an accident of fate. It wasn't a natural disaster or the act of a few madmen like 9/11. It was the people of the United States—a country and a people she'd believed in for her entire life—choosing this man to be our leader.

"These people are vandalizing democracy," she told me. "And he's the last president I'll ever have."

"Trump will be a one-term president," I assured her. "There's another president left in you."

I'm a lifelong Democrat. I consider myself politically aware and lean toward progressive policies, particularly on social issues. To stay current, I read the *New York Times* and visit the CNN website several times a day for updates. If there's a newsworthy event on television, I might watch it live. Sometimes, I look at highlights on the internet after it's over.

What I didn't (and still don't) do is subject myself to a constant stream of images and commentary from and about Donald Trump. I don't want it pounding in my brain when I go to sleep at night.

As Mom grew older, CNN and MSNBC were a constant presence in her life. And the news depressed her. Sometimes I'd counsel, "Look, we agree that things are bad. But you don't have to wallow in it. Watch something else on television."

"I like being well-informed on political issues," she'd counter. "I just hope I live long enough to see Trump lose when he runs for reelection."

Meanwhile, the aging process continued. Most people want to live a long life. Being old is less enticing.

Mom started using a walker when she went out. She got one of those pendants that elderly people wear around their neck with a button to push that connects to an operator in case of a fall or other incapacitating incident. Instead of her housekeeper coming in once a week, we arranged for her to be there four days a week from 2:00 PM to 7:00 PM. That way, she could cook dinner for mom and clean up before she left. The housekeeper was also responsible for accompanying Mom to the supermarket, dentist appointments, the hairdresser, and the like.

Then Mom started using a wheelchair when she went out.

"It is what it is," she said.

At the end of each visit, Dr. Kutnick repeated his caution to her: "Don't fall."

Reading was now my mother's primary daytime activity. I bought her an early printing of *Little House in the Big Woods* (which had been her favorite book when she was a child). She read it in a day.

"Boy, did that bring back memories," she said.

When Mom was ninety-three, she read in the *New York*

Times obituary section that an old acquaintance named Ben Heller had died.

"It's a strange feeling," she told me. "I knew Ben from the time we were kids. We went to Fieldston together. I remember, when we were twelve years old, our mothers drove us to Playland [a local amusement park]. I hadn't seen him since the last reunion. There were eight of us from our class who were still alive then. It can't be more than seven now."

"Someone has to be the last," I said. "Maybe it will be you."

Mom now felt weak much of the time. Her energy level was dropping like a stock on a long downward decline. Her morning telephone calls to me evolved from a cheery "I'm alive and well" to "I'm still here."

But she still found pleasure in her daily routine. She enjoyed being with family and friends. And there were times when she had a very good time.

Honey, Anne, and I would take Mom to Manor Beach Park (a forty-minute drive from the city and ten minutes from our old house in Larchmont) for picnics overlooking the Long Island Sound. In autumn, we'd drive through the turning leaves before stopping for lunch at the Larchmont Tavern (a restaurant Mom had gone to decades before).

Mom had always liked meeting new people, especially people whose backgrounds were different from her own. Over the years, I'd introduced her to a number of friends and acquaintances from the boxing side of my life. Once, I'd brought her to a press conference at Madison Square Garden to meet Don King. King went out of his way to charm her. Years later, Mom was at a Greek restaurant on the east side of Manhattan when a loud booming voice proclaimed, "It's Tom Hauser's momma!" It was King.

Now Mom was meeting fewer people. She still liked going out for lunch. But getting tickets in advance for lectures and other events was too much for her. Within that framework, it was important that she keep having experiences that gave her pleasure.

Enter Artie Pelullo.

Artie is a boxing promoter from Philadelphia. Some people mistake him as being just a big affable guy. He's more than that. He's very smart. Artie has lived his life on the right side of the law. Some of his relatives from earlier generations didn't. As a consequence of those family connections, Artie grew up knowing—drumroll please—Frank Sinatra.

So, I set up a lunch with Artie, my mother, and myself. Mom would have liked Artie under any circumstances. But talking with someone who actually knew Sinatra and the stories that Artie told her were proof positive for Mom that there would be more interesting people to meet and more good times ahead.

"I've had a wonderful life," Mom told Artie at the close of lunch. "The only thing I didn't get that I wanted was an assignation with Frank."

"I wish you'd told me that when Frank was alive," Artie responded. "We might have been able to set something up."

Afterward, I thanked Artie for coming.

"No, thank you," he said. "I had as much fun as your mom did. Whatever 'it' is, your mom has got it."

Mom had now reached a point in her life where she was always aware that "something" might happen and hoped that it wouldn't be more serious than anything that had happened before. She wasn't in pain. She didn't have an incapacitating disability. But she was tired most of the time. She accepted her condition. "I can live with this" joined "it is what it is" as a guiding principle.

There were poignant moments. She was extremely fond of her cousin, Bill Lehrburger, who lived with his wife in North Carolina. Mom had known Bill since they were kids. In 2019, he and Dinny came to New York to celebrate his ninetieth birthday and visited Mom at her apartment.

"This will be our last trip north," Bill told her. "The travel is just too much for us."

"It's very sad," Mom told me after they'd left. "Bill and I have been in each other's lives for ninety years. And I'll never see him again."

Then Mom started having vision problems. Her eyes tired after she read for a short period of time. She'd adapted well to each previous age-related limitation. This one was tough. Reading had been one of her greatest pleasures. I began ordering large-print books for her. After a while, they became difficult to read too.

"I keep thinking about all the good things that have happened to me in my life," Mom said. "I'm so lucky. But I feel like it's getting to that time."

The shadow of her mortality was an undercurrent in my thoughts too.

On Sunday, December 1, 2019, I arrived home after visiting Mom and checked my telephone answering machine. There was a message from Ed Brophy (executive director of the International Boxing Hall of Fame) asking me to call him. When I checked my email, there was a similar message asking me to give Ed a call.

Earlier in the year, my name had been placed on the ballot for induction into the International Boxing Hall of Fame for the first time. The public had been told that the names of the newest inductees would be announced on December 4. Like every nominee, I hoped I'd be chosen. Given the realities of the induction process, I doubted that I would be. Still . . . "Ed's not a sadist," I reasoned. "He wouldn't be calling to tell me that I didn't get in."

I called Brophy back and he congratulated me on being chosen for induction. There would be a news embargo until the inductees were announced as a group on December 4.

"Please, don't tell anyone," Ed urged.

I honored that request with one exception. It would have been cruel beyond words if Mom were to die without my telling her. So, I telephoned her and shared the news.

A month later, Mom lost one of the few friends she had who was older than she was.

Ellie Appleby's mind was still sharp. At age ninety-nine, she was able to take walks in the park. Her children were attentive. But her eyesight had faded badly, and she had other physical problems. She wasn't enjoying life anymore.

A year earlier, Ellie had asked Mom if Mom was interested in traveling to Switzerland with her to end their lives through assisted suicide.

"No way," Mom told her. "My traveling days are over. And I still love living."

Ellie and Mom were scheduled to have lunch together on a Saturday in early 2020. That morning, Ellie's housekeeper called. Ellie was in the hospital with an intestinal blockage and had two options. She could have an operation that she'd probably survive. Or she could do nothing in which case she would likely be dead within a week. She chose the latter and died five days later.

Ellie's death was another reminder to Mom of her own mortality. And she'd lost another friend.

Then I had (forgive the immodesty) a stroke of genius.

Mom couldn't read for long without her eyes getting tired.

CNN and MSNBC were becoming a bit much even for her. And there were times when it was hard to find a movie or something else on television that she liked. Saturday nights were particularly barren.

"I'm getting you an iPad so you can watch YouTube," I told her.

"Don't you dare."

"Trust me. I know your limitations. You'll enjoy it."

"Not a chance."

Mom had never learned how to use a computer. Or email. Her intellectual curiosity stopped short of anything technological. Robin had sent her a Kindle when her eyesight began to falter. That would have enabled Mom to read by enlarging the font on the screen.

"Tom can teach you how to use it," Robin said.

Tom couldn't teach her how to use it. The will to learn a new technology simply wasn't there.

I understood Mom's resistance. For years, I'd written by hand on lined yellow paper. And for years, friends had told me I was crazy. But I have limited technological skills and was intimidated by computers.

Then I had a telephone conversation with my brother's older daughter who was eight at the time.

"What did you do today, Cathy?"

"I taught Jessica how to use the computer."

Jessica was four. Recently, I'd complimented her on her ability to count. "You're very smart," I'd told her.

"I know," Jessica had responded. "And you know what else I know, Uncle Tom? Two plus two equals five."

This is embarrassing, I told myself. Jessica is now more computer literate than I am.

So, I learned how to use a computer. And it changed my life.

I said earlier that my mother had a remarkable mind and that she'd retained her full cognitive abilities as she grew older. I did not say that she had a gift for technology. Teaching her to use an iPad was, shall we say, an adventure.

Mom learned to open the iPad, push the start button, type in her passcode (her birthday, 12-28-25), and touch the YouTube icon on the screen to open the application.

Then she'd call me.

From that point on, I'd follow what she was doing simultaneously on my own iPad and give instructions.

Getting a cursor in the search box was challenging.

Mom was good at typing. Once we got the cursor in place, she could type in what she wanted to see (for example, "Frank Sinatra concert" or "Kennedy Center Honors"). But that was just the start.

"Touch the return key,"

"All right. I touched the return key."

"What do you see on the screen."

"Nothing."

"There has to be something on the screen. What do you see?"

"A box."

What's in the box?

"A picture of Frank Sinatra."

"Touch the picture of Frank Sinatra."

"The picture is bigger now. But I want to see Frank singing when he's older."

"No problem. Do you see an arrow in the upper-lefthand corner of the box?"

"No."

"What's in the upper-lefthand corner of the box?"

"An arrow."

"Okay. Touch the arrow."

All of which made it particularly satisfying one Saturday night when I came home, played the messages on my telephone answering machine, and heard Mom's voice: "Can you hear what I'm listening to? Frank Sinatra is singing and he's just the age I like him. I got it on my iPad all by myself."

The iPad and YouTube opened a whole new world for Mom. Saturday night was now "date night" with Sinatra singing just for her and a dozen or so concerts to choose from. She watched other performers and documentaries about people ranging from Winston Churchill and Albert Einstein to Sidney Poitier and Rex Harrison.

"I had a dream last night," Mom told me the morning after she'd watched a documentary about the last of the aforementioned subjects. "I was in a hotel room. The doorbell rang, so I opened the door. And it was Rex Harrison."

"Does this mean that Rex Harrison is now on the short list?"

"I guess so. He doesn't rank as high as Frank. But I was happy to see him. And he seemed happy to see me."

By the start of 2020, I was talking with Mom on the phone several times a day. There was our morning call, a second call in late-afternoon, and one more just before she went to bed.

On January 6, 2020, I called Mom around 5:00 p.m. This was one of the days when her housekeeper wasn't there.

Mom didn't sound right.

"Tell me about the Golden Globes last night," I said.

"That man. He got an award. You know who I mean."

"Which man?"

"He was, you know . . ."

I went over to Mom's apartment.

"Let's go to the emergency room," I said.

"I don't want to go to the emergency room."

Mom had her speech and full cognitive ability back now.

"I have an appointment for a check-up with Dr. Horbar [her internist] tomorrow. If we go to the emergency room, all that will happen is, I'll sit there for four hours and then they'll put me in a room overnight and I'll be there for three days while they run tests and put gunk in my hair before they let me go home."

"Why don't I call Dr. Horbar?"

"No! He'll tell you to take me to the emergency room. It happened. It's over. I'm ninety-four years old. I know what my situation is, and I don't want to go to the emergency room."

So, we didn't go to the emergency room. I arranged for Mom's housekeeper to spend the night. The following day, I went with Mom to see Dr. Horbar who told us that the incident had all the symptoms of a classic TIA, and that yes, if I'd called, he would have told me to take Mom to the emergency room, but that no harm had been done by not taking her there.

Two months later, COVID hit. Now Mom's life was further constricted. Someone who contracted COVID in 2020 had a two-percent chance of dying from it. For a 94-year-old woman, COVID could easily be a death sentence.

"If Obama was still president," Mom said, "the Republicans would be calling it 'the Obama virus.'"

Her world was less sunny now. She was likely to spend the rest of her life under the shadow of COVID. One of the restrictions that bothered Mom was not being able to go to the hairdresser. After being shut down for several months, the salon that she went to reopened with COVID protocols in place.

"You can't go," I told her.

"Why not?"

"It's not safe."

So, she didn't go. But not going made her unhappy. So finally, I gave my blessing and her weekly visits to the hairdresser resumed.

Growing old is hard. Not the minor aches and pains that become more common but don't change the way a person lives. Not the changes in appearance that accumulate over time until, one day, someone looks at a recent photograph and says, "Omigod! I look old." I'm talking about reaching a point in life where a person needs more and more help to do things—taking a box down from a shelf, changing a light bulb—that were once easy to do.

More and more, Mom was confronted with things that she couldn't do for herself. She knew she'd never wake up in the morning feeling rested and fully refreshed. Whenever she left her apartment, it would be in a wheelchair. She'd never walk leisurely in the park or dance again.

"Most people who are ninety-four aren't," she said.

Three months after turning ninety-four, Mom suffered another small TIA while she was on the phone with Anne Teall. She called to tell me about it afterward.

She was lucid.

"It makes even less sense to go to the emergency room now than after the last TIA," she said. "First, if I go, I'll probably get COVID. Second, because of COVID, they won't let you in with me. And third, they won't do anything."

She was speaking logically and sequencing well. So, we didn't go to the emergency room.

Several days later, there was an obituary in the *New York Times* for a high school classmate of Mom's named Steve Lieber who'd made a lot of money in finance and been a true philan-thropist.

"He wasn't a rich kid back then," Mom told me. "I liked him. We were in the same economics class. There were eleven boys and me and he was the smartest."

Mom's housekeepers started coming in at 10:00 a.m. instead of 2:00 p.m. on the four days a week that they saw her.

Then, in June 2020, there was another troubling incident. Mom didn't make her "I'm still here" morning telephone call. I telephoned her at ten and got the answering machine. A few minutes later, I called and got the machine again.

Mom had just hired a second housekeeper (who'd worked previously for Ellie Appleby) to help cover the expanded hours. The new housekeeper didn't have a key to Mom's apartment yet. But Mom had given me her mobile number. I called and the housekeeper said she'd been standing outside Mom's door for several minutes and had rung the doorbell three or four times. Mom hadn't answered.

"I'll be right over," I said.

Just then, Mom opened the door. She'd woken up at 9:30, gone into the kitchen, and was buttering a bagel when suddenly she felt weaker than she'd ever felt. It had been a struggle for her to get to the door to let the housekeeper in.

I went to Mom's apartment. She was cognitively sound and didn't want me to call any of her doctors. I'd brought a fingertip pulse oximeter with me (a COVID precaution) and checked her oxygen level and pulse rate. Both were normal.

I stayed with Mom for the next few hours. She got progressively stronger. The housekeeper spent the next few nights at her apartment.

Mom's doctors were unanimous in saying that she could keep living alone "if that's what she wants."

It was what she wanted.

"I love living," Mom told me. "But if I go to sleep tonight and don't wake up, that's all right. I've had a wonderful life."

And she still had her sense of humor.

"Are you going to fine me a hundred dollars for not calling you this morning?" she asked.

"No. You get a pass on this one."

~

Life was now difficult for Mom in many respects. But there was also joy.

Each day was marked by a stream of thoughtful acts by people who boosted her spirits. Her apartment was a safe haven. She planted roses and zinnias on the balcony. Friends visited regularly for lunch. A woman named Arlynn Greenbaum came weekly and played bridge with Mom on their iPads whenever they got together. Mom's own iPad use expanded to videos that ranged from Zero Mostel in *Fiddler on the Roof* to speeches by Malcolm X.

Over the years, Mom had met most of my friends and was interested in meeting new ones as they came into my life. "Your mother is amazing," was a refrain I often heard after someone had joined us for lunch. "She's a lot of fun," a friend who was a psychotherapist offered.

How many people in their mid-nineties are referred to as "fun." And by "fun," we aren't talking about someone who elicits smiles because she's feisty at an advanced age.

"I'm smarter now than when I was young," Mom said when I passed along the compliment. "I've learned some things along the way."

When Mom turned ninety, she'd proclaimed, "Forty years ago, happiness was a carton of cigarettes and a bottle of vodka. Now it's a week's worth of bagels and cinnamon challah knots."

But as she moved into her mid-nineties, she didn't enjoy food as much as she had before. Her weight dropped from 125 to 110 pounds.

Anne sent everything from chicken noodle matzoh ball soup to croissants to fatten her up. Mom picked the carrots out of soup and ate the croissants with jam. Every few weeks,

Robin would ask Mom what she most felt like eating for dinner and ordered it online for delivery from a local restaurant.

I made a point of letting Mom dictate the menu for our Sunday lunches. She also developed a taste for walnut chocolate chip cookies and raisin sticky buns from a bakery called Levain.

One Sunday morning, I stopped at Levain on the way to Mom's apartment. Two young women were behind the counter taking orders. Another customer (a woman who I'd guess was in her fifties) ordered a raisin sticky bun the same time I did.

"I'm sorry," one of the young women told us. "There's only one raisin sticky bun left. What would you like us to do?"

"It's for my seventy-eight-year-old mother," the other customer said.

"My mother is ninety-four."

"For real?"

"For real."

"Okay. You can have it."

I also got points for what Mom called a "miracle" purchase online. Mom was sentimental about family history. From time to time, I'd Google her parents and others on the family tree. There wasn't much beyond the occasional obituary and wedding announcement.

One afternoon, I typed in "Elise Lehrburger" (Mom's mother's maiden name) on Google. My grandmother had gone to public high school in Massachusetts for three years followed by a year at an institution called The Madame Archard School in Brookline.

There, on eBay, was a brass medallion with a lilac-colored enamel design on one side. The other side had a silver finish with the words engraved, "Presented by the Madame Archard School on completion of her studies to Elise Lehrburger 1921."

The medallion was listed by a dealer in Tennessee. I have

no idea how it got there.

"I can't believe it," Mom said when I gave her the medallion. "I just can't believe it."

She put the medallion on top of her bureau, and it stayed there until she died.

In September 2020, Mom cast her absentee ballot for Joe Biden. In November, her spirits were lifted when he was elected President of the United States.

"I just crossed another thing off my bucket list," Mom said.

She was content with her life. She was pain-free. She lived with her problems, not in them.

"It would be nice to be two years younger," she told me. "But you can't always get what you want. One good thing about being old is that I know I won't die young. So many people are killed in accidents and by diseases when they're too young to die."

She wasn't a burden. She made very few demands and was grateful whenever anyone did anything for her. Each time I went to her apartment, she made a point of telling me how much she appreciated my being there.

People still looked forward to seeing her. A lot of us were happier because she was in our lives.

She savored her memories. They gave texture and meaning to her life. "Very few people have memories as wonderful as I do," she said.

She wanted to keep living. But she was at peace with the idea of going to bed one night and not waking up.

"I love every day," she told me. "But I don't want to go like Si or Bud."

I started ending our telephone conversations with "goodnight" or "talk with you later." I didn't want to say "goodbye."

Mom turned ninety-five.

We expanded the hours that one or the other of her two

housekeepers worked from 10:00 AM to 8:00 PM every Monday through Saturday. If there was a Sunday that I couldn't go, Honey covered for me.

Mom started to feel particularly unsteady if she had to go to the bathroom during the middle of the night. We bought a commode and put it by the side of her bed. She'd always meticulously kept her home, whether it was the house in Larchmont or her apartment in New York. The commode was not an attractive piece of decor.

The carpeting in the apartment was thirty-one years old, a bit frayed and stained in a few places.

"Leave it the way it is," Mom said.

The was a crack in the paint on her bedroom wall, the result of leakage from a pipe in the apartment above. Mom didn't want to go through the hassle of having it plastered and painted over. Finally, I put a strip of masking tape over the crack and painted the tape white. The color didn't quite match the rest of the wall. But to Mom's fading eyesight, it was a match.

She woke up tired each day and was very tired by late afternoon.

"It comes with being ninety-five," Mom said. "It's life. It's nature."

Now and then, I'd bring up the idea of someone living with Mom on a fulltime basis. I didn't pressure her. I knew she wanted to live alone. And her doctors said it was all right for her to continue living alone. So, it was her choice.

Always, Mom would say, "I'd rather live alone for as long as I can."

In early 2021, COVID vaccinations began. Mom very much wanted to be vaccinated. She still wanted to live. I navigated the online process and got appointments for us at Metropolitan Hospital.

The first dose was easy to facilitate. Dose number two was more complicated. We had appointments but a snowstorm interrupted the delivery pipeline. When we arrived at Metropolitan Hospital, there was a line of people waiting to be vaccinated that stretched down a corridor and looked to be about two hours long.

Mom, in her wheelchair, was not a happy camper.

"We're already here," I told her. "Let's get on line and see what happens."

I wheeled Mom to the end of the line and started back toward the front desk to ask how long the wait would be.

"Excuse me. Are you Thomas Hauser?"

The question came from a young man who was wearing hospital scrubs and appeared to be an orderly.

"Yes."

"I loved your Ali book."

"Thank you. Are you a boxing fan?"

"Big-time."

There was a pause as he looked down the line and weighed what to say next.

"Get the old lady and come with me."

So, I went back to the end of the line, got the old lady, and wheeled Mom to where the orderly was waiting. He led us to the front desk, told one of the women on duty "they're cool," and brought us inside. Ten minutes later, we were vaccinated.

I don't believe in cutting lines. This was an exception. And thank you, Muhammad Ali.

When Mom worked at *The New Yorker*, she'd developed a fondness for the poetry of Ogden Nash. Nash was known for writing light verse. His first poem for *The New Yorker* was published in 1930. Hundreds more followed. After my grandfather died, Mom and I had read one of Nash's poems titled "The Middle" together:

> *When I remember bygone days*
> *I think how evening follows morn*
> *So many I loved were not yet dead*
> *So many I love were not yet born*

Mom wasn't in "the middle" anymore. But she felt connected to the generations that came after her as much as she had to the generations that came before. My brother's daughters were a particularly important presence in her life.

Cathy (my brother's first child) was born in 1983. She married and moved from Oregon to Montana, where her husband (Nick) manages a store that sells and installs flooring, kitchen cabinets, and the like. Their children (Reece and Ruby) made Mom a great-grandmother.

Jessica (my brother's younger daughter) was born in 1987 and, after serving in the Peace Corps, moved to New York. She now lives in New Jersey and oversees media relations for the litigation department at a large Manhattan law firm. She and her husband (Bayo) married in 2020. Living to see their first child was one of Mom's goals. Simon (named after my father) was born on February 13, 2021.

Mom's sister had died in 2009 after a long battle with cancer. In 2021, Mom's brother passed away.

Ed had been a success story in his early years. He graduated from Harvard and followed in my grandfather's footsteps as a member of the law review at Columbia. But there came a time when he had trouble navigating the world at large. Ed lived with my grandparents until he was thirty and my grandfather told him that it was time for him to live on his own. After poor experiences at several law firms, he settled into a decades-long career as an administrator with the Securities and Exchange Commission.

Mom and Ed had been close. Then he started drinking heavily. There came a time when he was drunk almost every night. That was a problem. He and Mom were pleasant to each other at family gatherings. They talked on the phone now and then. But as they aged, they drifted apart. And both of them knew it.

It was a running joke that, if Ed knocked over his water glass at dinner, Mom would think, "That's disgusting. Look how drunk Ed is." But if I knocked over my water glass, she'd say, "Look how considerate Tom is. He's cleaning the table."

When the pandemic began, Ed didn't shave for more than a year. That was a matter of convenience (he disliked shaving) and, I suppose, a statement of some sort. But the longer and shaggier his beard got, the worse it looked, particularly when there was food in it.

In late August 2021, Ed was diagnosed with terminal multiple-organ failure. His internist told my brother (who was close with Ed) to set up home palliative care and not bring him back to the hospital.

"Let him watch television. Make him as comfortable as possible. He has about thirty days before nature takes its course."

The day Ed died, I went with Mom to his apartment. We were the last family members to see him alive. Mom took his hand. He was her little brother again. At first, Ed wasn't aware of who she was. His eyes had a haunted lonely look. Then his eyes changed. It seemed like he recognized her and that it was comforting to him that she was there. He died several hours later.

Mom had been four years older than Ruth and eight years older than Ed. Now she was the only one of the three alive.

Three days before Mom's ninety-sixth birthday, we celebrated what would be her final Christmas. Jessica, Bayo, Simon, and Bayo's parents joined us at Mom's apartment. I'd been assigned catering duties which included cooking the turkey.

"Everyone loved putting the Christmas tree up," Mom said as she reminisced about long-ago Christmases. "But no one liked helping me take the tree down."

Mom and I were now talking on the phone four times a day. There was the morning call after she woke up, an afternoon check-in, an evening call around the time the housekeeper left, and a final chat right before Mom went to bed. The calls were short or long depending on what we had to say.

Everything that Mom did took longer than before. Refilling her pill box once a week had become a time-consuming activity. If Mom dropped a pill on the floor, first she had to find it. Then it was an effort to get down on the floor to pick it up. She'd lower herself to her knees, take the pill in her hand, steady herself on a piece of furniture, and lift herself back up.

When Mom was ninety, one could see that once upon a time she'd been a beautiful woman. At ninety-six, she simply looked old.

"I don't remember imagining when I was young what I'd look like when I was wrinkled and gray," she told me. "Now I look in the mirror and say to myself, 'Eleanor, you're almost a century old.'"

She began talking more about her mortality but not in a morbid way. She sensed that she was nearing the last stop on her long life journey.

"When it's time, it's time," Mom said. "Everything I get now is extra."

She romanticized from time to time about seeing her parents, Alan, and other people she loved in heaven. She didn't believe. But it was nice to fantasize. "And someday, maybe I'll see you there too," she told me.

The joy of life and the shadow of death were complementary, not conflicting, themes for her.

And she kept current. That's for sure.

"I'm watching the college football championship game tonight," I told her during one of our early-evening conversations.

This was a woman who had no interest in football. Most likely, the only football she'd watched on television in her entire life was when she turned on the TV on a Sunday evening to watch *60 Minutes* and the late-afternoon football game on CBS was running long.

"Alabama against Georgia," Mom responded.

"How in the world do you know that?"

"They were talking about it last night on CNN. I know a thing or two about a thing or two."

I knew that, one day, I'd see her and then never see her again. I wanted her to have a soft landing when the end came.

"I'd do anything for you and give you anything you asked for," Mom told me during one of our Sunday lunches. "You know that, don't you?"

"I do. And knowing that is better than anything you could do for me or give me."

Her dignity and spirit remained intact.

"I'm glad that I got to eat raspberries fresh off the bush and pick roses in the backyard . . . I've had it all. I've lived a wonderful life . . . Life doesn't owe me anything. I've been lucky from the day I was born."

And then my mother fell.

Chapter VIII

S hortly before midnight on Saturday, March 5, 2022, I was getting ready for bed when the telephone rang.

"I fell and hurt myself," Mom said.

"Where are you?"

"On the floor outside the bathroom."

"What hurts?"

"My back."

"Does your head hurt?"

"No."

"Don't move. I'll be over as soon as I can."

I put on my clothes, went downstairs, and got a taxi fairly quickly. The ride to Mom's apartment took about fifteen minutes but seemed longer. For most of that time, I was on the phone with Mom, doing my best to reassure her.

I was nervous and a bit scared.

This is real, I told myself.

When I got to Mom's apartment, she was in her nightgown, lying on the floor outside her bathroom.

Each night before she went to bed, Mom brushed her teeth

and used the toilet one last time. This time, she'd slipped and fallen on her way out of the bathroom. There was a pendant around her neck, but she hadn't pushed the help button. Instead, she'd dragged herself along the floor to her walker outside the bathroom door, knocked the walker over to get her portable phone, and called me.

I knelt down on the floor beside her. She looked like an old, weak, wounded woman.

"Let's do some checks. Do you know where you are?"

"On the floor in my bedroom."

"Who's the president of the United States?

"Joe Biden."

"Tell me what happened."

"I was walking out of the bathroom and slipped."

Her mind was clear.

"Can you wiggle your fingers? . . . Now your toes . . . Hands and arms . . . Feet and legs . . ."

There was no sign of paralysis.

She didn't want me to call 911.

"It's Saturday night. The emergency room is full people who overdosed on drugs. All that will happen is, I'll lie on a gurney for six hours. I want to stay here."

It was my decision. I was totally responsible for her wellbeing.

"Okay, we'll stay here."

I lifted her up and got her into bed. When she moved, her lower back hurt. If she didn't move, there was no pain.

I gave her two extra-strength Tylenol and put a glass of water on the night table beside the bed.

"Could you put a coaster under the glass so it doesn't leave a ring," she instructed.

She was still Mom.

I slept in the living room on the sofa. Lying there, I

wondered if this was the start of the end game for my mother. And if it was, how long and hard would it be for her. I woke up to go to the bathroom once during the night and looked in on her. She was sleeping soundly and breathing regularly.

On Sunday morning, I called Mom's internist, explained what had happened, and described her symptoms.

"Sunday isn't a good day to go to the emergency room," I told her when the call was over. "Dr. Horbar's mother is the same age you are. He says to stay in bed, and we'll see how you feel in a day or two."

That was in line with Mom's thinking and my own. But instead of the previous ten-hours-a-day, six-days-a-week schedule, she now needed 24/7 help. One of Mom's housekeepers stayed with her while we transitioned to more experienced care.

Two of Mom's friends gave us referrals. Three new caregivers began rotating hours. Two of them were exceptionally capable nurturing women. The third did her job.

Up until she fell, Mom had enjoyed living. There were struggles but she was happy to be alive. Despite her infirmities, she had what people call a "good" old age. Now she sensed that those days had come to an end and the rest of her life would be marked by the inability to control her surroundings, weakness, and physical pain.

"I've lived long enough," she told me.

For the first time in her life, she wanted to die.

I was Mom's health care proxy (as I'd been for my father). When she was well, she had expressed her wishes in no uncertain terms. There are people who tell their doctors, "I want to live. Do everything you possibly can to keep me alive for as long as you can." That wasn't Mom.

"If I'm unconscious," Mom had told me, "don't bring me

back if I can't be myself. And I don't mean crap like Jim or Lise saying, 'It's still Mom inside.'"

The question now was whether we could get Mom back to where she was before she fell. And if not, what would her new baseline be?

I went to see Mom every day. She wasn't in pain when she was lying in bed or sitting in a chair. It hurt a lot when she moved. There was no point in subjecting her to the disruption of bringing her to a facility for an X-ray or MRI. Whatever the result, she wasn't having surgery.

An orthopedist examined her via video conferencing and prescribed a painkiller. "We'll start slowly and hope for healing," he told her. "We'll do what we can to stop the pain. At ninety-six, you're not worrying about becoming an addict."

A neurologist came to the apartment and determined that Mom's neurological functions were sound.

But she sensed that this was the end game.

"The chances of my getting better are as good as the chances of Frank Sinatra coming over for dinner tonight," she told me. "Both would be nice and neither is going to happen."

Sixteen days after she fell, Mom's condition took a turn for the worse. Honey, Anne, and I were at her apartment for lunch. Mom wasn't up to joining us in the dining room, so she'd stayed in bed. While we were there, she began to feel increasingly and dramatically weak.

I hadn't given up hope that Mom would recover to the point where she had what she felt was an acceptable quality of life. I called 911. An ambulance brought us to Lenox Hill Hospital. I sat in back with Mom and a paramedic. Listening to an ambulance siren from the back of the ambulance with someone you love is very different from standing on the sidewalk as an ambulance speeds by.

Mom was lucid in the emergency room. She gave an

administrator her name and date of birth but struggled with extended conversation. At one point, she looked at me and, overlooking my many flaws, told the attendant "perfect son."

Then, lying on a gurney in a holding area, she went into delirium.

"Why are you wearing my coat?" she asked me.

I didn't know what to say.

"I want to see the baby."

That made no more sense to me than my wearing Mom's coat.

"I want to see the baby. Please, let me see my baby."

And I realized that Mom had gone back more than seventy years in time and was reexperiencing the last of her miscarriages.

My three-year-old self flashed through my mind. I was in bed, looking out my bedroom door at my mother in her sea-green nightgown. She was in distress, but I wasn't old enough to understand what was happening.

Mom tried to climb off the gurney.

I held her in place until her agitation subsided.

After tests, it was determined that Mom's condition had been brought on by dehydration and a urinary tract infection.

We got a private room to make her stay in the hospital more comfortable. She struggled for words from time to time as she came back from the brink. But for the most part, talking with her was like talking with her before the fall. During one of my visits, she recalled visiting her own mother in the hospital decades earlier.

"I was the one in the chair you're sitting in now," Mom told me. "And my mother was the one lying in bed."

A CT-scan showed that she'd suffered a compression fracture in her lower back when she fell.

"It will heal with time," one of the doctors said.

"I'm done. It's wrong that I can't die when I want to."

"That's not your choice," the doctor told her.

After eight days, we brought Mom home from the hospital. That necessitated moving furniture around to accommodate a bulky hospital bed. Medical clutter replaced the carefully calibrated order of her once bright, cheerful apartment.

Mom had been assigned a physical therapist and social worker but didn't want sessions with either of them.

She asked for her Jo Malone Wild Bluebell Cologne because, in her words, "I don't want to smell like an old lady."

She was depressed but preferred being at home to the hospital. Her fear was that her condition was "the new normal" and would drag on for months. Visitors lifted her spirits a bit.

Coordinating Mom's care was a challenge. There were constant updates with doctors, family, and friends . . . Making sure there was someone with her at all times . . . Going from drug store to drug store to fill a new prescription because we needed the drug now, not tomorrow . . . The seemingly endless stream of taped messages and holds before speaking with someone in the medical establishment on the telephone.

And the fraudulent spam calls that elderly people get all the time kept coming. Only now when someone said they were calling from a medical supply company, I couldn't just hang up. I had to listen to determine if the call was authentic.

I'd seen Mom cry when people she loved died. If she cried about her own plight, I never saw it.

My brother had come to New York to see Mom when she was in the hospital and stayed for several days after she came home. One afternoon, Jim and I were in the kitchen talking about Mom. We started crying and hugged each other. More than the ritual male-greeting hug.

I don't remember our doing that before.

Later that day, we recounted the moment for Mom.

"Our love for you has brought us closer," I told her.

"Maybe that makes these past few weeks worthwhile," she said.

Mom was sleeping reasonably well at night. She rested quietly or dozed off for much of each day.

She was adamant in saying that she didn't want to live anymore.

Nine states and the District of Columbia have right-to-die statutes. But they're difficult to implement and limited in application to people who live in those states.

"New York is a progressive state," Mom told me. "Why can't New York allow what Oregon allows?"

The answer to that question lies in the heartfelt moral and religious beliefs of some people. And if you'll forgive a moment of cynicism—the medical expenses mount astronomically for someone who's dying. I doubt very much that the institutions making money off the current system want to change it.

I'd told Mom when she was well that I'd never let her suffer a prolonged brutal end game.

Now what?

I knew enough people that I could probably get hold of a life-ending drug. But there could be ugly legal consequences if things evolved the wrong way.

And there was a moral issue. Did I have the right to put myself above the law to help end my mother's life?

Was my moral uncertainty a cop out? Maybe. But putting oneself above the law to end a life is a slippery slope.

So, when Mom said again that she wanted to die, I told her, "I'll make a deal with you. Let's do everything we can for the next month to see if you can get to a place where you want to keep living. And if you can't get there, then we'll decide what to do next."

I felt helpless. I was buying time. I didn't want to fail Mom when it mattered most.

Death was on the horizon now. Mom was pain free, which was good. Some days, she slept most of the time. Other days, she was alert and reasonably strong.

"Sometimes it's enough to lie back and let people love you," I told her.

As I spoke those words, I was spooning soup into her mouth as she'd done for me when I was a year old.

We were doing everything we could to make her as comfortable as possible. But the only time she was really comfortable was when she was asleep. You let someone go out of love.

One afternoon, I was sitting by her bed and put a Frank Sinatra concert on the iPad. It was one of his last. "Old Blue Eyes" was "Very Old Blue Eyes" by then. But he was still Sinatra. And he could still sing.

Glass in hand, Sinatra toasted his audience with the benediction, "May you all live to be a hundred years old and may the last voice you hear be mine."

Then he started singing.

Lying on her back, eyes closed, Mom lifted her arms and began moving them in time with the music. In her mind, I think, she was dancing. I hoped that each breath she took would be her last.

Two days later, she was gone.

On Sunday, April 10, five weeks after Mom fell, Honey and I were on our way to her apartment when I got a text from the caregiver who was with her.

"Please come as soon as possible."

And I knew.

Mom was lying in bed when I got there. Her eyes were

open but sightless. She wasn't breathing. I checked for a pulse. Nothing.

In that moment, I knew with startling clarity that my mother was dead. I'd rather not have that image of her in my mind. But it will be there forever.

You hear people say, "Oh, she looks so peaceful," or "He looks so calm and serene."

No! Dead people look dead.

Whatever comes next, I told myself, it's happening now.

Chapter IX

I sat with Mom on a chair next to the bed for a while. Then I pulled a sheet up over her head. That seemed like the right thing to do.

I felt an enormous sense of relief that her suffering was over. I knew I'd miss her. The thought of a ship returning safely home to harbor after a long voyage passed through my mind.

I called my brother first. Then my sister.

I waited before calling 911. There was no sign of life when the emergency medical technicians arrived, but they tried to revive Mom anyway. I showed them her health care proxy, but the lead EMT said it wasn't operative in situations like this. I needed a different form that had just been issued by the state.

He lifted Mom out of bed, put her down on the floor, and started pressing down on her chest.

"Stop!" I shouted.

"Sorry, it's the law."

"Would you want someone doing this to your mother?"

"No. But I have to follow the law."

This was why I'd waited before calling 911. During the last

year of her life, Mom had told her housekeepers, "If there's a problem, don't call 911. Call Tom."

After a few minutes of trying to bring Mom back from the dead, the EMT gave up.

I telephoned Anne, Robin, and Mom's internist.

Several police officers came and went.

I spoke with Cathy and Jessica and telephoned more of Mom's friends.

Someone from Riverside Memorial Chapel removed Mom's body from the apartment.

Just before I left, I took a shopping bag out of the foyer closet and dumped all of Mom's jewelry in it to bring home for safekeeping. This wasn't organized packing. I went through bureau drawers and cabinets and threw every piece I found into the bag.

Mom had shown me where everything was. Now I heard her saying, "Stop! What are you doing! You're getting everything mixed up."

I added two family heirlooms—a Tiffany vase that had belonged to Mom's grandparents and an old silver Kiddish cup that had been in the family for generations.

The precaution was well-founded. Later that month, someone broke into Mom's apartment and stole three small Japanese wood carvings off a shelf in the foyer. I reported the theft to building management and the police, but there was no serious follow-up.

The day after Mom died, I was very tired. The world felt different without her.

Several years earlier, she'd told me that, when the time came, she wanted an obituary in the Sunday edition of the *New York Times*. We'd worked out the wording together with a few blanks to be filled in after her death.

It took a while to make my way through the *New York*

Times labyrinth to find out how to place a paid obituary ("death notice"). Classified ads, I learned, were the entry point. One week after Mom's death, the obituary ran:

> *Hauser, Eleanor Nordlinger: Died peacefully on April 10 at age 96 after a long and fulfilling life. She was a loving wife and companion to Simon Hauser, Bernard Nossiter, and Alan Raphael, and a warm presence in the lives of her parents (Elise and Harry Nordlinger), her children (Thomas, James, and Elise), four grandchildren, three great-grandchildren, and countless other family members and friends. Interment is private. At her request, in lieu of flowers, contributions should be made to The Ethical Culture Fieldston School in Riverdale, New York, or Planned Parenthood Federation of America.*

The condolence letters from Mom's friends started coming in.

"I loved your mom. I will always cherish our friendship . . . I have her picture on my dresser so I see her every day . . . She was a very special woman . . . You were so lucky to have had her as your mother for all these years . . ."

Five days after Mom died, I picked up her remains at Riverside Memorial Chapel. For most of her life, she'd said that she wanted a traditional burial. But in her later years, she changed her mind and said she preferred cremation with her remains interred at Mount Pleasant Cemetery in Hawthorne, New York, where her parents were buried.

"And I want a simple box like you got for Si," she told me. "Nothing fancy."

So, I'd gone out and bought a decorative heavy-cardboard box with green leaves on a white background and showed it to Mom when I was at her apartment for lunch.

"Does this meet with your approval?"

"It's just what I wanted. Thank you."

I was surprised by how little I grieved in the aftermath of her death. In the past, when friends suffered losses, I'd assured them that someday they'd smile whenever they thought of their loved one. Here, the smiles came sooner than I'd expected. I felt very strongly that Mom's time had come. Being at peace with her death wasn't something I could bring about as an act of will. It simply was.

The day that I picked up Mom's remains at the funeral home and was dealing with all of the emotions and responsibilities that came with her death, my printer broke.

What could I do? Tell people, "It's been a hard week. My mother, who I loved more than anyone else in the world, died on Sunday. And my printer just broke." I'd sound like a lunatic.

Mom hadn't wanted a formal funeral or memorial service. Just a simple interment with the people she loved most gathered there to bid her farewell.

Five years earlier, I'd updated the paperwork for Mount Pleasant Cemetery. My grandfather had bought a lot there where he and my grandmother were buried and there had been space for three more graves. But the paperwork hadn't been tended to since the early 1980s.

"Better to do it now than when we need it," I'd told Mom and my uncle. They agreed, so I'd filled out the necessary forms and submitted the required affidavits. My uncle had been cremated and interred there one year earlier.

Mom's remains were in a closet in my apartment.

"Don't forget to bring Mom," I told myself on the day of her interment.

She had made a list of the people she wanted invited to the cemetery. My brother couldn't come because he'd contracted COVID and was home in Oregon. But he participated via

FaceTime as did Robin (who'd undergone oral surgery that morning). My sister and her children chose not to attend.

There were fourteen of us at the cemetery: Cathy (my brother's older daughter), Nick (her husband), Reece and Ruby (their children), Jessica (my brother's other daughter), Bayo (her husband), Simon (their seventeen-month-old son), Oye and Judy (Bayo's parents), Anne, Honey, Jim Lehrburger (Bill's son), Karen Lehrburger (Jim's wife), and myself.

The ceremony began with Sinatra on an iPhone ("You Make Me Feel So Young"). Then we took turns reminiscing about Mom.

As Cathy and Jessica were speaking, I thought back to the little girls they'd once been. Their first sleepovers at my apartment. Spending hours with them in the Barbie room at FAO Schwarz after I'd told them we'd go there and they could pick out anything they wanted up to fifty dollars each (which went further in the early 1990s than it does today).

"Ellie gave me a roadmap for growing old," Robin remembered.

"I'm incredibly sad right now," Anne said. "I loved Ellie a lot. But thinking about her will always comfort me."

Then the youngest generation had its say.

Reece had just turned thirteen. "Grandma was one of the nicest people ever," he said. "She did everything she could to make people happy. She'd talk with me about her life when she was a kid and she talked with me about grown-up things like politics. She made me feel like she loved me so much."

Ruby, eleven, recounted locking horns with Grandma at her apartment.

"I told Grandma, 'You're not my boss. Mommy is my boss.' And Grandma told me, 'In my apartment, I'm the boss.'"

"What did you like most about Grandma's apartment?" Ruby was asked.

"That it was Grandma's."

Simon slept through most of it. Someday when he's old enough to understand, people will tell him about his great-grandmother and show him photos of them together.

After everyone spoke, we shoveled dirt on top of Mom's remains and put flowers on her grave. She would have liked the ceremony.

❧

One could build a TV reality series around what it's like for a son who's the executor of his mother's estate to navigate the waters after his mother has died.

I cancelled her credit cards and subscription to the *New York Times*, put a hold on her bank and brokerage accounts, arranged for pick-up of the hospital bed, and went to the post office to ensure that her mail was forwarded to me.

Dealing with her telephone-internet-cable-TV service was an adventure. After keying in numbers and listening to music, I was put through to a customer representative who listened as I explained that my mother had died and that I wanted to close her account. I got the scripted "please accept our condolences for your loss" speech. Then, after being put on hold again—

"I'm sorry, sir. You're not listed as an authorized representative on your mother's account. Could you get her on the line so she can confirm that you're authorized to close her account?"

I'm not making that up. She actually said that.

"I want you to think about what you just said," I told her. "And then ask yourself if you want me to tell your supervisor that you said it or would you rather just close the account?"

I began getting calls from debt collection agencies representing credit card companies. None of Mom's cards had an outstanding balance of more than seven hundred fifty dollars. I explained to each of the collection agents that the bills would be paid once I was formally named as executor by the Surrogates Court. And I asked that they contact me by mail only. Under the law, the collection agents were required to honor that request.

But one of the agencies kept calling. Finally, I got the emotionally satisfying idea of asking the caller to "hold on for a moment" while I went to the kitchen to make a cup of coffee, came back several minutes later, and said, "I'm sorry this is taking so long. I can play some music for you if you'd like."

At that point, the collection agent hung up on me.

I hired the same law firm that drafted Mom's will to oversee probate. Prior to the pandemic, a certificate designating me as the executor of her estate would have been issued by the Surrogates Court within three weeks. Now it took three months. Once the designation came, I opened an estate account, transferred Mom's assets to it, and paid her bills. There was a long stream of paperwork with forms to fill out and trips to the bank for medallion signatures when a notary signature wouldn't suffice.

Mom's will contained a clause giving her diamond engagement ring to me and several other belongings to Jim and Lise. Distributing the rest of her possessions was my responsibility. Years earlier, she'd told me that I'd inherit most of her personal property and should do whatever I thought was appropriate with it. I'd asked for guidelines as to how she might want things to be distributed, and she gave me several lists. Her will provided that, after the pieces mentioned above were distributed, all of her other possessions were mine with the understanding that I could keep what I wanted and give away the rest as I saw fit. It also stated that any lists she might have given me didn't have to be followed.

I shared the lists with my brother and sister and followed

them down to the smallest detail. Most of the items that Mom listed were designated for family. But there were exceptions. Alan had given my mother a gold wedding band. Mom asked that I give the ring to Robin. Bud had given Mom a gold ring embedded with tiny diamonds. Mom wanted that ring to go to Honey. Anne got a gold watch and long gold chain.

I divided the rest of Mom's belongings as though she were looking over my shoulder.

Emptying my mother's apartment was a huge task. I'd pretty much known what was there. Now I went through all of her belongings, drawer by drawer, closet by closet, deciding what to give to each family member, what to give to friends, what to give to charity, and what to throw out.

Four huge closets, a bureau, and a large chifforobe were filled with clothes. God, she had a lot of clothes! Cathy and Jessica took some, and I gave some to Anne, Robin, and Honey.

Mom had kept all of the condolence cards that she received after my father, Bud, and Alan died. They were in the same drawer as her high school diploma.

She had close to a thousand books. Jim, Cathy, Jessica, and I took some. Then I invited Arlynn Greenbaum (who was a reader like Mom and had come almost every week to play bridge with her on the iPad) to take whatever books she wanted.

Mom had asked me to "give something nice" to Jim and Karen Lehrburger. I gave some of her earrings to Karen and, going through Mom's books, found an ideal gift for Jim—a copy of *The Poetical Works of Alfred Lord Tennyson* with an inscription that read, "Souvenir to Miss Tillie Frank, Boston 7/3/89, S. L. Lehrburger."

In 1889, Simon had been courting Tilly. They were Mom's grandparents and Jim's great-grandparents.

So many things in Mom's apartment took me back in time.

To celebrate her sixtieth birthday, I'd written a poem that began:

> *Sixty years ago today on a cold December morn*
> *To Elise and Harry Nordlinger, a little child*
> *was born*

The poem was in a drawer with a *New York Times* review of a novel I'd written thirty years earlier about a plot by a wealthy industrialist to manufacture nuclear weapons for sale to third-world countries. Mom had taken a pen and, doting mother that she was, bracketed the words, "Few writers currently in action would be able to match the mounting tension of *The Hawthorne Group*."

A copy of a eulogy that Anderson Cooper wrote for his mother was on Mom's desk. In part, it read, "The last few weeks, every time I kissed her goodbye, I'd say, 'I love you, Mom.' She would look at me and say, 'I love you, too. You know that.' And she was right. I did know that. I knew it from the moment I was born, and I'll know it for the rest of my life."

Mom had asked me to print out the eulogy. When I gave it to her, she told me, "If you really do write a book about me, I hope you'll write how much I love you and how much you mean to me."

Once I decided who got what, my mother's belongings had to be packed and shipped. Then I disposed of what was left. Old financial files and other papers were thrown out. One of Mom's attendants asked for her wheelchair, walker, and other medical equipment to ship to a charity in Guyana.

There are dealers who buy the leftover contents of apartments, broom-clean the premises, resell some of what they take, and throw out the rest. Here, after the best of Mom's belongings were given to family and friends, there was little worth reselling, so no dealer was interested.

Charities don't pick up in New York City unless a donation has significant monetary value. No one will remove a thousand ordinary books from an apartment unless they're paid for the removal. And there was furniture that no one wanted.

With Honey's help, I spent day after day filling heavy-duty 55-gallon garbage bags with clothes and other items that we brought to a Salvation Army drop-off center. Other bags were left by the garbage chute on Mom's floor. The superintendent was paid to dispose of what was left.

At times, I had the unsettling thought that someday someone will be going through my belongings the way that I was going through Mom's.

As weeks and then months passed, there were times when I took a break from writing or whatever else I was doing and thought instinctively, "This is a good time to call Mom."

A new Frank Sinatra concert was posted on YouTube. His voice had faded. He couldn't remember the names of composers and arrangers. But he sang like only Sinatra could sing, and he was the age that Mom liked him when she was in her own very old years. I missed her in that moment. I wanted to call and tell her, "There's a treat for you on your iPad tonight."

The "I should call Mom" moments grew fewer and further in between.

December marked the first time in my life that I didn't spend Christmas with my mother.

Now I walk around my own apartment and see so many things that remind me of her. Meals at my grandparents' apartment were shared beneath an eight-foot-tall grandfather clock that once belonged to my great-great-grandparents. My grandmother gave it to me when my grandfather died. But my parents liked it, and I said they could keep it in the house in Larchmont. After my father suffered his stroke and the house was sold, Mom said it was time to put the clock in my apartment.

Mom's grandparents had an elaborately inlaid wood table that was built in the 1890s. It was on the list of things that Mom wanted me to have. Over the course of a century, the wood had dried out and cracked. I had the table restored. After the work was done, I wanted to call her and say, "You won't believe how good the table looks."

So many things have a story behind them that someday will be lost to time. I'm a book junkie. I have almost five thousand books in my apartment. One of them is a copy of *Second April* by Edna St. Vincent Millay that belonged to my grandfather. An inscription on the inside of the front cover reads, "To my dear boss and friend on his sixtieth birthday with deep affection. Jerry."

I might be the only person alive who remembers that Jerry was my grandfather's secretary.

There are scrapbooks I've kept over the years that track my own life . . . Two Teddy bears that were in my crib when I was an infant . . . A nut dish that I carved out of a block of wood during my first summer at sleepaway camp . . . So many things of significance to me will have no meaning to others as time goes by.

Like Mom, I've lived a privileged life. I'm part of the most privileged generation ever, a generation born in the right place at the right time with a combination of security and comfort unmatched since the beginning of time. I'm fortunate to have had the family I've had and the friends I've made. I've never suffered from hunger or been in an environment where I was beaten or otherwise abused.

I've been blessed with good health, been pain free, and

slept well throughout my life. I've gone swimming on hot summer nights, walked through the woods with autumn leaves at their peak, gone fishing, and actually caught some fish. I've seen the Pyramids and Sphinx; London, Paris, Rome, Florence, and Venice; the Sistine Chapel and Taj Mahal; Mount Everest, Machu Picchu, and animal migrations in East Africa. I've watched the sun rise over the Atlantic Ocean and set over the Pacific. I've read *Anna Karenina* and *The Grapes of Wrath* and came of age during the golden age of rock and roll.

I was at Madison Square Garden the night that Marilyn Monroe sang "Happy Birthday" to John F. Kennedy.

Before Mom's death, I almost never thought about my own passing. Her being alive was a buffer against having to confront my own mortality. My father was only seventy-six when he died, younger than I am now. But I have significantly different medical markers than he did.

None of us is promised tomorrow. I know that. But in my mind, my own death was far in the future. Psychologically, Mom's longevity extended my own horizon. Regardless of what actuarial tables might say, I could tell myself that I was likely to live for twenty years after Mom died. There was no rational basis for thinking that way. I just did.

Now the clock is ticking on me. I'm the oldest living person in our family. Someday the sun will rise without me.

In 2018, when I updated the paperwork for the family plot at Mount Pleasant Cemetery in Hawthorne, I went through the ancestral scrapbook that my grandfather kept and also old documents I'd taken from my father's files when we emptied the house in Larchmont. When I did, I found deeds for three more cemetery lots that dated to the late 1800s.

Two of the deeds were on the Nordlinger side of the family for lots in Beth El Cemetery and Salem Fields Cemetery in

Brooklyn. The third (on my father's side) was for a lot in Washington Cemetery, also in Brooklyn.

Seven months after Mom died, I decided to visit the cemeteries. I went to Beth El and Salem Fields first. It was unseasonably warm for November. Winding footpaths spread across the undulating ground like a complicated maze. There were more trees than I'd expected. The autumn leaves were at their peak.

The Beth El family lot had nine filled graves and one open plot. The Salem Fields lot had five filled graves and five open plots. The monuments and footstones were remarkably well-preserved. It's likely that no one had visited them since my grandfather died in 1976.

Then I went to Washington Cemetery where my father's maternal grandparents (Sophia and Solomon Jaskowitz), one of his uncles, and two of his aunts were buried. I know next-to-nothing about them.

A woman who worked in the cemetery office checked her records and told me that they were buried in Cemetery 5, Post 463, Rows 1 and 2. "But some sections of the cemetery are so old that there might no longer be grave markers," she warned.

Most of Cemetery 5 was filled with tightly spaced stone markers a century old. Grass more than a foot high had been recently cut and lay around headstones and footstones like mulch on the ground.

The Jaskowitz grave markers weren't there, which seemed odd since earlier headstones dating to the 1800s were in place in neighboring plots. More troubling, several rows of four-foot-tall, thick black-marble headstones installed during the past twenty years encroached incongruously on some of the older grave sites (including the lot where I was told the Jaskowitz headstones had been).

I had the feeling that the Jaskowitz headstones had been broken down to make room for new arrivals.

A small number of men and women live on in the pages of history. As time passes, most of us are forgotten. People who were once vibrant and alive are reduced to memories in the minds of those who knew them. Eventually, they're known only as faces in photographs and names on a family tree.

As years pass, there will be fewer and fewer people who remember my mother. I'm writing now so that, years from now, she won't be one of the millions upon millions of people who are gone and forgotten after they die. This book is a more suitable marker for her than the footstone on her grave.

I knew my mother best as an older woman. That's the lasting image I have of her. Writing about Mom when she was young reminds me that there was a time when her entire life lay ahead of her. That remarkable journey has come to an end. But she lived longer and better than 99.999 percent of the people who ever lived. She understood that life is a marathon, not a sprint, that it's the process of becoming, and that all of us have within us the potential to be better people than we are.

Mom didn't believe in an afterlife in the traditional sense. Neither do I, although I suppose that continuing on in some recognizable form after death as we know it would be no more remarkable than being born to begin with. She believed that immortality lies in how we're remembered and how what we do during our lives changes the world and affects other lives after we're gone.

My mother will always be part of who I am. I'm grateful for the many years that I had her in my life. I know she was grateful that I was in her life too. She used to say, "I don't regret anything I've done for people, only the things I didn't do." There's nothing I wanted to say to my mother or do for her that I didn't get to say or do.

I rarely have pleasant dreams. Or if I do, I don't remember them. Most of the dreams I remember are pretty grim. Occasionally, a particularly bad dream penetrates my consciousness like a shard of glass.

Six weeks after Mom died, I had a dream. A joyous dream that I vividly recall. It's now firmly fixed in my mind and has supplanted the image of Mom lying in bed on the day she died . . .

Mom is in a bed in a large room with glass walls on a beach. It's a sunny day with a blue sky and gentle breeze. The room is empty except for the bed, which is facing the water. The tide is rolling gently in and out of the room so that the bed is resting in several inches of water. Mom, her late sixties or early seventies, looks healthy and vibrant.

"I didn't think this would happen," I tell her. "But you're well again."

"I don't believe it," Mom says. There's elation in her voice.

"It's true. You'll be going home."

About the Author

Thomas Hauser was born in New York and attended both college and law school at Columbia. After graduating from law school, he clerked for a federal judge before spending five years as a litigator at the Wall Street law firm of Cravath Swaine & Moore.

Since then, Hauser has authored books on subjects ranging from professional boxing to Beethoven. His first book—*Missing* —was nominated for the Pulitzer Prize, Bancroft Prize, and National Book Award, and served as the basis for the Academy-Award-winning film starring Jack Lemmon and Sissy Spacek. *The Beethoven Conspiracy*—Hauser's thriller about the search for a lost Beethoven symphony—won the Prix Lafayette, awarded biannually in France to the outstanding book by an American. Subsequently, Hauser co-authored *Final Warning*:

The Legacy of Chernobyl, again demonstrating his ability to explain and bring to life events of complexity and importance, an ability which has secured his reputation as a responsible and reliable social critic. The film version of *Final Warning* starred Jon Voight and Jason Robards.

Hauser's most celebrated work to date is *Muhammad Ali: His Life and Times*—the definitive biography of the man who was once the most famous person on earth. The British edition was honored with the William Hill Book of the Year Award in England. Subsequently, Ali and Hauser co-authored *Healing: A Journal of Tolerance and Understanding* and criss-crossed the United States, meeting with student audiences on their subject. For their efforts to combat bigotry and prejudice, they were named as co-recipients of the Haviva Reik Award. More recently, Hauser authored *Muhammad Ali: A Tribute to The Greatest*.

Hauser's award-winning investigative articles and testimony before the United States Senate Committee on Commerce, Science, and Transportation have been hailed within the boxing industry as a significant force for change. On nine occasions, articles he has written have been designated as the "best investigative reporting of the year" by the Boxing Writers Association of America. In 2004, the BWAA honored him with the Nat Fleischer Award for Career Excellence in Boxing Journalism.

In December 2019, it was announced that Hauser had been selected for boxing's highest honor: induction into the International Boxing Hall Fame.

Hauser's books are read worldwide in twenty languages. He has written articles for *The New Yorker*, *The New York Times*, and numerous other publications. He lives in Manhattan.

More By Admission Press

Looking for your next great read?
Visit www.admissionpress.com

Made in United States
North Haven, CT
07 May 2024

52213832R00096